Keto Cookbook

YUMMY

Keto Essentials, Keto Bread, Keto Desserts, Keto Snacks to Boost Brain Health, Prevent and Reverse Disease

Shanice Johnson

Introduction

Good health and a dietary routine, are both closely interlinked to one another. Back in 1921, owing to the importance of the food in human life and its health, a new dietary approach was discovered, which was named as Ketogenic diet. This fancy word came into existence when experts discovered the importance of ketosis in human metabolism and how it can be enhanced to improve both the physical and mental health of a person. Thus experiments were conducted to determine the effects of carbohydrates and fats separately on the human body. Surprisingly, fats, when taken in isolation, proved to be far healthier than carbohydrates. It was discovered that these fats in the absence of carbohydrates are responsible for accelerating ketosis in the body. The idea of a ketogenic diet then witnessed a drastic increase in its popularity as the harms of the sugars or carbohydrates were brought forth to the world. In this cookbook, we shall see how to avoid those sugars in our daily routine while managing to enjoy similar flavors. Different sections of recipes are designed to provide a variety of bread, snacks, and desserts. Since avoiding flours and sugars are the toughest part of a ketogenic diet, these recipes are designed specially to keep those ingredients out of your life while giving you perfect substitutes.

Chapter 1

Everything you need knows about the ketogenic diet

The concept of a ketogenic diet can be broken into three different parts. First, the method then the effects and finally its benefits. The method describes what the diet is and what it allow or does not allow to eat, the second part discusses what role it play in ketosis and what the ketosis actually is and then finally the benefits it can bring to human health.

The Ketogenic diet, concept, and benefits

At first ketogenic diet came out as a natural and organic treatment to Alzheimer and Parkinson's but as the professionals found out its wide spectrum health effects, it became more popular and greatly acceptable even by the general public. The idea of a ketogenic diet actually fought against all the prevailing myths which earlier accused fats of being the major cause of all health problems. It turned actually the opposite. Fats alone can't cause much harm until they are taken in excess, along with a huge amount of carbs. If we remove the carbs from the diet and focus more on the fat intake, it can provide promising health effects to the body.

The diet was named after a natural metabolic process "ketosis" due to its close relationship with the process, in fact, a direct relation. It is that process that organically happens in the body when a person is fasting, or he is falling short of the available blood glucose. In such a condition, to meet the required energy levels, excess fats present in the body are metabolized to release sufficient energy. Where ketones are produced as the byproduct of this process they also aid in preventing and treating mental illnesses like epilepsy, Parkinson's, or Alzheimer's. The essential formula of this low carb diet stayed the same over the past decades, that is to maintain a low carb and high-fat diet, but the method to such a dietary approach became clearer today due to better knowledge, research, and experiences of the past. Scientists and their fellow nutritionists have come out with a limit of 50 grams or less of carbohydrates per day to initiate ketosis. For this threshold to maintain we need to remove all the lentils, sugars, grains, legumes, milk, honey, high carb vegetables and fruits from the diet. Though all of these ingredients are basic energy sources, they can be replaced with fat-based sources like cheese, ghee, cream, butter, oils, etc.

Consumption of low carb and high-fat diet also results several other health benefits. Firstly, it is effective in preventing insulin resistance which is a condition suffered by diabetic type II patients. It is highly recommended to treat obesity; as a low carb diet allows the consumption of the deposited fats in the body. It also helps in providing lasting energy and prevents cardiovascular diseases. A sugar-free diet also ensures a cancer-free life.

What to Eat & What Not to Eat on a Ketogenic Diet

The challenge of the ketogenic diet is the constant struggle of distinguishing between the low carb and high carb ingredients. Since there are several processed food products available in the market, it is difficult to choose a carb-free option if we don't carry a list of Keto-friendly items in our hands. Down below is a precise list of the relevant ketogenic items which are low in carbs.

List of Keto-Friendly Food:

Seeds and Nuts:
Seeds and dry nuts do not contain a high dose of carbohydrates, and a balanced intake of these nuts and seeds can be taken on a Keto diet including the Pumpkin seeds, pistachio, almonds, walnuts, pecans, etc.

Keto-Friendly Vegetables
All low carb vegetables are Keto-friendly. Unfortunately, there is not a single yardstick to categories such as vegetables. We can look for the number of the carb's vegetables have. Generally, all the vegetables grown above the ground contain lesser carbohydrates like vegetable greens, leeks, asparagus, chilies, lemon, etc. Other than this onion, tomatoes, ginger, garlic, zucchini, etc. are also Keto-friendly vegetables.

Ketogenic Fruits:
There are several fruits which are full of sugars, and they can't be taken on this diet. Other than those the low carb fruits like blueberries, avocado, strawberries, raspberries, blackberries, coconut, cranberries, etc. are all allowed on the ketogenic diet.

Meat Items:
There is no restriction on protein intake; therefore, meat in any form is completely allowed on a ketogenic diet. Meat contains only proteins and fats, so they make a good part of a ketogenic diet. Whether it's the seafood, poultry: chicken, turkey, duck; beef, mutton, lamb, pork, etc. every meat is allowed on a diet.

Dairy Items:
Most of the dairy products are Keto-friendly except the "Milk," since milk is a raw item, it contains high traces of carbohydrates. However, when the milk is processed to get cheese, cream, cream cheese, and yogurt, etc, the carbohydrates are broken down into other by-products. Therefore, all these products are allowed on the ketogenic diet. Instead of milk, we can use the following plant-based milk substitutes.
Soy milk
Hemp milk

Almond milk
Coconut milk
Macadamia milk

Ghee, butter, and eggs can also be enjoyed on a ketogenic diet plan.

All Fats:
There is no limitation on the consumption of fat. Therefore any plant-based oil and animal-based ghee are completely allowed on this diet. Some of the commonly used cooking oil include olive oil, avocado oil, sesame oil, and canola oil.

Keto-Sweeteners:

Fear of cutting down the sweetness from their meals is what hit every ketogenic dieter the most. But the diet only restricts the carb intake not stops you from adding sweetness by using other substitutes. There are several Keto-friendly sweeteners available in the market today, including the following.

Erythritol
Monk fruit sweetener
Stevia
Swerve
Natvia

Food to Avoid on a Ketogenic Diet:

There are several items of everyday use which are full of the carbs. Naturally, all of them needs to be avoided on the Ketogenic diet. It's not just the sugars which should be crossed off the list; there are several other ingredients not suitable for a low carb diet as follows

1. Legumes:
Legumes like all beans, lentils, and chickpeas, etc. are the underground parts of the plants where they store most of the food in the form of carbohydrates. Therefore, none of the legumes are Keto-friendly, and they all should be completely avoided on this diet.

2. Grains:
All Edible grains are a good source of carbohydrates, like rice, wheat, millet, barley, etc. Grains are therefore strictly forbidden on a ketogenic diet. Food products obtained and processed from these grains are also not allowed like all-purpose flour, wheat flour, rice flours, chickpea flour, etc. The high carb grain flours can be replaced with:
1. Coconut flour
2. Almond flour

3. Fruits:
Fruits including oranges, banana, apples, pineapple, pomegranate, pears, watermelon are all very rich in sugars. Do not use these fruits on a ketogenic diet. all the Extracts and juices of these fruits should also be avoided.

5. Sugar:
All sugars are carbohydrates whether its glucose, fructose, or maltose. Therefore, sugars should be avoided completely, including white sugar, granulated, confectionery, baking, brown, sugar, etc. Products containing a high dose of sugar are also not allowed like processed food and beverages.

5. Tubers:
Tubers are including most of the underground vegetables like potatoes, beetroots, yellow squash, and yams. They all are not good for a ketogenic diet as they contain a high amount of starch, meaning carbohydrates.

6. Dairy:
Animal milk, including cow, and goat milk is completely prohibited on this

7. Sauces and Syrups:

Ketchup, maple syrup, chocolate syrups, dates molasses, honey, etc. which contain sugars in high amounts are also prohibited on a ketogenic diet. Replace the ketchup with a sugar-free one and use sugar-free chocolates for the recipes.

Major types of gluten-free Ketogenic flours

Flours are an essential ingredient to bake aromatic bread and cakes. Unfortunately, all grains based flours are full of carbs, so they cannot be used in such recipes. However, there are other ketogenic options which provide good taste and texture to all the bakes and desserts:

Almond Flour

This flour is obtained from almonds when they are finely ground into a powder and is commonly used for baking ketogenic bread and desserts. There are two popular varieties of the flour available for use that is the blanched and unbranched varieties. The first is obtained from blanched and peeled almonds, whereas the second one is produced by grinding and processing the raw nuts. That is why the blanched flour is finer in texture, appears pale in color and most commonly used for bread and desserts. The unblanched flour has a coarse texture and appears brownish in color. It has a grainy texture and gives a crumbly bakes and bread, whereas the blanched flour offers fluffy texture to the bread.

Almond Meal

Almond meal tastes and looks different from the low carb almond flour. A meal is coarser and is not ideally used for bread and cakes. The almond meal is used to add texture to the recipes. It is often used in granola or crumbly cookies or nutty bars.

Walnut Meal and other Nuts flour:

All nuts based meals are suitable for ketogenic meals. Ground walnut or other nuts ground is good to use as a gluten-free option. Since every nut gives a different texture, they are only recommended when a certain texture is needed in the recipe. Nuts infuse their unique flavor into the bakes and desserts so they should be used accordingly. To obtain the nut's meal, simply grind them into a powder after drying them properly. Since all seeds vary in their properties, it is recommended to opt market packed nut flours.

Psyllium Husk

The psyllium husk is obtained from the seeds of a plant named Plantago ovata. Being a husk it is a soluble fiber. It is available in the form of coarser husk form and also as the flour which is much finer in texture. The psyllium husk powder is good to use in low carb desserts, bread, and other confectioneries due to its light and airy grains; it gives the bakes a soft and fluffy texture

Coconut Flour

Coconut flour is another low carb flour which is obtained from the dehydrated coconut flesh. The dried flesh is finely ground which turns it into flour. This flour has a nice texture and a unique taste. The texture of the coconut flour is not similar to the wheat flour; it is denser and can soak more moisture than all-purpose flour. Due to this quality, extra liquid is added to the coconut flour while making doughs and batter to get the wheat-like texture. This flour can also make clumps in a batter; which why a good beater is recommended when it used.

Flaxseed flour and Flaxseed Meal

Flaxseeds can also be used instead of gluten flours. They are rich in fats, minerals, vitamins, and antioxidants which makes them a healthy substitute to wheat-based flours. It is good for heart health and the human digestive system. Flaxseed can both be used in the form of meal and flour for the ketogenic diet. Flaxseed flour and meal are used in muffins, bread, and cookie. The flaxseed meal is coarser than the flour just like almond meal. Both varieties are easily available in grocery stores.

Chapter 2

Guide to low carb sweeteners used in baking

The low carb sweeteners are not ordinary sugars; they all are sourced from different plants and compounds, so they taste differently and carry their intensity of sweetness. So having a basic understanding of these sweeteners is imperative to cook a nice bread or Keto dessert. Following Keto friendly sweeteners are commonly prescribed by the experts.

Erythritol

Erythritol is basically sugar alcohol which is not really a sugar but a dietary fiber that tastes sweet and easily digested and excreted by the body without increasing its carbs and caloric intake. Erythritol is present naturally in different plants, including melons, grapes, and mushrooms in some amount. For commercial use as a sweetener, it is made from fermented corn. Erythritol is about 70 percent as sweet as the table sugar. It brings the cooling sensation to the tongue when consumed in a large amount. Some people experience some digestive issues with this sweetener like bloating or loose stools. On the other hand, the sweetener is good to prevent cavities and dental plaque.

Stevia

Stevia is a naturally sweet substance that and the liquid form. The is extracted from a planted named stevia grown in South America. Due to its sweetness and the low carb properties, it is a commonly used Keto-friendly sweetener. Stevia is available both in powder form and liquid form. The stevia is a good substitute to sugar as it offers intense sweetness, but it does not taste like sugar rather licorice-like taste. And it is 200 times sweeter than table sugar. A tsp of stevia is equivalent to a cup of sugar.

Sorbitol

Sorbitol is another sugar alcohol that has a low glycemic index. It offers a good sweet taste with a little lasting after taste. The sweetener provides 2.5 calories in one gram which makes it a good low caloric option other than the erythritol. The sweetener contains 55 percent of the sweetness when compared to the sweetness of the table sugar. Its low glycemic value makes it suitable for all the individuals suffering from diabetes. Naturally, it is present in pears and apples and even produced inside the human body in some amount. Sorbitol has been in use for a decade by the diabetics due to its composition. It is also popular for its medicinal effects. It should only be consumed less than 20 grams per day.

Xylitol

Another sugar alcohol, xylitol is a Keto-friendly low carb sweetener which is naturally present in vegetables and fruits in some amount. It is commercially produced from birch trees or the corn cobs. It is a frequently used sweetener for making sugar free mouth wash and chewing gums etc. Xylitol is only a low carb sweetener, not a zero carb substitute, so it is only recommended in a limited amounted, not more than 20 grams per day. When consumed only 50 percent of the xylitol in absorbed in the body via the small intestines, so it hardly raises the blood sugar levels or the insulin levels. It is equally sweet as the table sugar but only provides half the calories the same amount of sugar provides.

Coconut sugar

The coconut sugar is also known by the name of coconut palm sugar since it is extracted from the coconut palm tree. The sap extracted from the palm tree is sugary and sweet, so it is processed to make natural sugar. It is essentially different from other palm trees extract sugars. The coconut sugar is available in granulated form and also in brown form. When it comes to ketogenic diet coconut sugar is often seen as a sugar substitute but certainly not a popular option since it is too sweet.

Sugar alcohols and their glycemic index

Sugar alcohols are the naturally existing compounds that taste sweet but do not contain much of the calories and the high carbs. As per their chemical composition, they are dietary composition. All alcohol sugars have a very low glycemic index which makes them a suitable option for a ketogenic diet. The glycemic index of an ingredient indicates how much sugar or the carbs it contains. Glucose has the highest glycemic value 60; all other sweeteners are then compared to this stand value to measure their glycemic values. The following are the sugar alcohols that have a low glycemic index value.

Sugar Alcohols	Glycemic Index
Xylitol	12
Glycerol	5
Sorbitol	4
Lactitol	3
Isomalt	2
Mannitol	2
Erythritol	1

- **Other Sweeteners**

Swerve is another Keto-friendly sweetener not only used in baking, but also for ice creams, fat bombs, mousses, and other desserts. Swerve sweetener is available in a variety of forms from brown, white swerve powder to the granulated form. Monk fruits sweetener, Natvia, and Sukrin are some other options which can be used in the ketogenic desserts.

sugar	1 tsp	1 tbsp	1/4 cup	1/3 cup	1/2 cup	1 cup
erythritol	1 1/4 tsp	1 tbsp + 1 tsp	1/3 cup	1/3 cup + 2 tbsp	2/3 cup	1 1/3 cup
xylitol	1 tsp	1 tbsp	1/4 cup	1/3 cup	1/2 cup	1 cup
swerve	1 tsp	1 tbsp	1/4 cup	1/3 cup	1/2 cup	1 cup
stevia	-	-	3/16 tsp	1/4 tsp	3/8 tsp	3/4 tsp
liquid stevia	3/8 tsp	3/8 tsp	1 1/2 tsp	2 tsp	3 tsp	2 tbsp

sukrin:	1 tsp	1 tbsp	1/4 cup	1/3 cup	1/2 cup	1 cup

Chapter 3

Ketogenic Breakfast Bread

Pumpkin Gingerbread

Preparation time: 10 minutes
Cooking time: 60 minutes
Servings: 24
Ingredients:
3 cups swerve
1 cup of vegetable oil
4 eggs
2/3 cup water
1 (15 ounces) can pumpkin puree
2 teaspoons ground ginger
1 teaspoon ground allspice
1 teaspoon ground cinnamon
1 teaspoon ground cloves
3 1/2 cups almond flour
2 teaspoons baking soda
1 1/2 teaspoons salt
1/2 teaspoon baking powder

How to prepare:
First, prepare the oven and preheat it at 350 degrees F.
Layer two loaf pans of 9x5 inches.
Whisk sweetener with eggs and oil in a mixing bowl with a beater until smooth.
Stir in water, ginger, pumpkin, clove, and allspice cinnamon then mix well.
Take another bowl and mix flour with salt, soda and baking powder in this bowl.

Pour in the eggs mixture and mix well to form the bread batter.

Divide this batter in the loaf pans and bake them for 1 hour approximately.

Slice and serve.

Nutritional Values:
Calories 165
Total Fat 14 g
Saturated Fat 7 g
Cholesterol 632 mg
Sodium 497 mg
Total Carbs 6 g
Fiber 3 g
Sugar 1 g
Protein 5 g

Blueberry Zucchini Bread

Preparation time: 10 minutes
Cooking time: 50 minutes
Servings: 12
Ingredients:
3 eggs, lightly beaten
1 cup of vegetable oil
3 teaspoons vanilla extract
2 1/4 cups swerve
2 cups shredded zucchini
3 cups almond flour
1 teaspoon salt1 teaspoon baking powder
1/4 teaspoon baking soda1 tablespoon ground cinnamon
1 pint fresh blueberries
How to prepare:
First, prepare the oven and preheat it at 350 degrees F.
Grease four mini loaf pans with cooking oil.
Take a large bowl and add baking powder, salt, flour, cinnamon, and baking soda.
Beat eggs with sweeteners, vanilla, oil, and eggs in a separate bowl.
Add the dry flour mixture and blend until smooth.
Fold in zucchini and berries then divide the batter in the mini loaf pans.
Place the filled loaf pans on a baking sheet and bake for 50 minutes approximately.
Serve.

Nutritional Values:
Calories 107
Total Fat 9.3 g
Saturated Fat 4.8 g
Cholesterol 77 mg
Sodium 135 mg
Total Carbs 2.6 g
Fiber 0.8 g
Sugar 9.9 g
Protein 3.9 g

Blanched Keto Bread

Preparation time: 10 minutes
Cooking time: 45 minutes
Servings: 12
Ingredients:
cooking spray
7 eggs, at room temperature
1/2 cup butter, melted and cooled
2 tablespoons olive oil
2 cups blanched almond flour
1 teaspoon baking powder
1/2 teaspoon xanthan gum
1/2 teaspoon sea salt
How to prepare:
First, prepare the oven and preheat it at 350 degrees F.
Grease a silicon loaf pan with cooking oil.
Now whisk eggs in a mixing bowl until creamy for 3 minutes.
Stir in olive oil and butter, then blend again until smooth.
Add baking powder, xanthan gum, salt, and almond flours in another mixing bowl.
Stir in the eggs mixture and mix well to make a thick batter.
Spread this bread batter in the prepared pan evenly.
Bake the batter for 45 minutes approximately until golden.
Slice and serve.

Nutritional Values:
Calories 106
Total Fat 5.9 g
Saturated Fat 1.5 g
Cholesterol 3 mg
Sodium 313 mg
Total Carbs 8.5 g
Fiber 3.2 g
Sugar 3.7 g
Protein 4.7 g

John's Avocado Bread

Preparation time: 10 minutes
Cooking time: 20 minutes
Servings: 12
Ingredients:
cooking spray
2 cups almond flour
1 teaspoon salt
1 teaspoon baking powder
1 teaspoon baking soda
1/2 cup butter, softened
3 avocados, mashed
1 cup swerve
2 large eggs
1/4 teaspoon vanilla extract
1 tablespoon almond milk
1 cup chopped walnuts
1/3 cup sugar-free chocolate chips
How to prepare:
First, prepare the oven and preheat it at 350 degrees F.
Grease a 9x4 inch loaf pan with cooking oil.
Now whisk the flour with baking soda, baking powder and salt in a bowl.

Separately beat sweetener with butter in a mixer until smooth.

Stir in flour mixture then add walnuts, chocolate chips, and avocado mash.

Mix well until smooth then spread in the loaf pan.

Bake for 20 minutes or more until golden.

Slice and serve.

Nutritional Values:
Calories 192
Total Fat 11.8 g
Saturated Fat 3.9 g
Cholesterol 135 mg
Sodium 187 mg
Total Carbs 4.1 g
Fibre 0.1g
Sugar 2.1 g
Protein 5.9 g

Dutch Caraway Rye Bread

Preparation time: 10 minutes
Cooking time: 35 minutes
Servings: 8
Ingredients:
2 cups light rye flour
2 cups almond flour
1/4 cup almond milk
2 tablespoons caraway seeds
2 teaspoons flaked kosher salt, crushed
1 3/4 cups warm water
2 teaspoons swerve
3/8 teaspoon active dry yeast

How to prepare:
Start by mixing flour with rye flour, gluten, sat, caraways seeds and milk in a bowl.

Beat yeast, water, and sweetener in another bowl and let it sit for 5 minutes.

Add this mixture to the flour mixture and mix well to make a smooth dough.

Wrap the dough with a plastic wrap and keep it aside for 18 hours.

Spread the dough in a greased loaf pan.

Bake for 35 minutes approximately at 500 degrees F.

Slice and serve.

Nutritional Values:
Calories 121
Total Fat 12.2 g
Saturated Fat 2.4 g
Cholesterol 110 mg
Sodium 276 mg
Total Carbs 3 g
Fiber 0.9 g
Sugar 1.4 g
Protein 1.8 g

1-Minute Keto Bread

Preparation time: 10 minutes
Cooking time: 01 minute
Servings: 01
Ingredients:
1 egg
2 teaspoon coconut flour
1 pinch baking soda
1 pinch salt
How to prepare:
First grease a suitable ramekin dish or a coffee mug with coconut oil. Whisk in all the bread ingredients and mix well them until smooth. Place the batter in the ramekin in the microwave for 1 minute at High settings.
Serve immediately.

Nutritional Values:
Calories 272
Total Fat 18 g
Saturated Fat 5 g
Cholesterol 6.1 mg
Sodium 3 mg
Total Carbs 4 g
Fiber 3 g
Sugar 4 g
Protein 0.4 g

Zucchini Bread

Preparation time: 10 minutes
Cooking time: 60 minutes
Servings: 24
Ingredients:
3 cups almond flour
1 teaspoon salt
1 teaspoon baking soda
1 teaspoon baking powder
1 tablespoon ground cinnamon

3 eggs
1 cup of vegetable oil
2 1/4 cups swerve
3 teaspoons vanilla extract
2 cups grated zucchini
1 cup chopped walnuts
How to prepare:
Start by preparing and preheating the oven at 325 degrees F.
Layer two 8x4 inches pan with cooking oil and flour.
Mix all the dry bread ingredients together in a separate bowl.
Beat the wet bread ingredients together in another bowl until smooth.
Stir in flour mixture, zucchini and walnuts, then mix well.
Divide the zucchini batter in the pans.
Bake them for 60 minutes approximately.
Slice and serve.

Nutritional Values:
Calories 201
Total Fat 12.2 g
Saturated Fat 2.4 g
Cholesterol 110 mg
Sodium 276 mg
Total Carbs 4.3 g
Fiber 0.9 g
Sugar 1.4 g
Protein 8.8 g

Maine Pumpkin Nutmeg Bread

Preparation time: 10 minutes
Cooking time: 50 minutes
Servings: 24
Ingredients:
1 (15 ounces) can pumpkin puree
4 eggs
1 cup of vegetable oil
2/3 cup water
3 cups swerve

3 1/2 cups almond flour
2 teaspoons baking soda
1 1/2 teaspoons salt
1 teaspoon ground cinnamon
1 teaspoon ground nutmeg
1/2 teaspoon ground cloves
1/4 teaspoon ground ginger

How to prepare:
Start by preparing and preheating the oven at 325 degrees F.
Layer three 7x3 inches pans with cooking oil and flour.
Mix all the dry bread ingredients together in a separate bowl.
Beat the wet bread ingredients together in another bowl until smooth.
Stir in flour mixture then it all well until smooth.
Divide the pumpkin batter in the pans.
Bake them for 50 minutes approximately.
Slice and serve.

Nutritional Values:
Calories 151
Total Fat 12.2 g
Saturated Fat 2.4 g
Cholesterol 110 mg
Sodium 276 mg
Total Carbs 3.2 g
Fiber 1.9 g
Sugar 0.4 g
Protein 8.8 g

Sour Cream Avocado Bread

Preparation time: 10 minutes
Cooking time: 60 minutes
Servings: 15
Ingredients:
1/2 cup butter, melted
1 cup swerve
2 eggs

1 teaspoon vanilla extract
1 1/2 cups almond flour
1 teaspoon baking soda
1/2 teaspoon salt
1/2 cup sour cream
1/2 cup chopped walnuts
2 medium avocado, mashed

How to prepare:
Start by preparing and preheating the oven at 325 degrees F.
Layer a 9x4 inches pans with cooking oil and flour.
Mix all the dry bread ingredients together in a separate bowl.
Beat the wet bread ingredients together in another bowl until smooth.
Stir in flour mixture, avocado and walnuts, then mix well.
Add the walnuts batter in the pans.
Bake them for 60 minutes approximately.
Slice and serve.

Nutritional Values:
Calories 173
Total Fat 16.2 g
Saturated Fat 9.8 g
Cholesterol 100 mg
Total Carbs 9.4 g
Sugar 0.2 g
Fibre1 g
Sodium 42 mg
Protein 3.3 g

Almond Meal Bread

Preparation time: 10 minutes
Cooking time: 40 minutes
Servings: 9
Ingredients:
1/2 cup butter
2/3 cup swerve
2 eggs
1 cup almond milk
1/2 teaspoon baking soda
1 cup almond meal
1 cup almond flour
1/2 teaspoon salt
How to prepare:
Start by preparing and preheating the oven at 375 degrees F.
Layer an 8 inches pan with cooking oil.
Mix all the dry bread ingredients together in a separate bowl.
Beat the wet bread ingredients together in another bowl until smooth.
Stir in flour mixture, then mix well.
Spread the flour batter in the pan.
Bake them for 40 minutes approximately.
Slice and serve.

Nutritional Values:
Calories 251
Total Fat 24.5 g
Saturated Fat 14.7 g
Cholesterol 165 mg
Sodium 142 mg
Total Carbs 4.3 g
Sugar 0.5 g
Fiber 1 g
Protein 5.9 g

Pecans Sour Cream Bread

Preparation time: 10 minutes
Cooking time: 60 minutes
Servings: 32
Ingredients:
1/4 cup swerve
1 teaspoon ground cinnamon
3/4 cup butter
3 cups swerve
3 eggs
3 avocados, mashed
1 (16 ounces) container sour cream
2 teaspoons vanilla extract
2 teaspoons ground cinnamon
1/2 teaspoon salt
3 teaspoons baking soda
4 1/2 cups almond flour
1 cup chopped pecans
How to prepare:
Start by preparing and preheating the oven at 300 degrees F. Layer four 7x3 inches pans with cooking oil.
Mix all the dry bread ingredients together in a separate bowl.

Beat the wet bread ingredients together in another bowl until smooth.
Stir in flour mixture, and pecans, then mix well.
Divide the pecans batter in the pans.
Bake them for 60 minutes approximately.
Slice and serve.

Nutritional Values:
Calories 255
Total Fat 23.4 g
Saturated Fat 11.7 g
Cholesterol 135 mg
Sodium 112 mg
Total Carbs 2.5 g
Sugar 12.5 g
Fiber 1 g
Protein 7.9 g

Cherry Scones

Preparation time: 10 minutes
Cooking time: 17 minutes
Servings: 8
Ingredients:
2 cups almond flour
1/3 cup swerve
1 teaspoon baking powder
1/4 teaspoon baking soda
1/2 teaspoon salt
8 tablespoons unsalted butter, frozen
1/2 cup dried cherries
1/2 cup sour cream
1 large egg
How to prepare:
After setting the oven in the lower middle portion of the oven preheat it at 400 degrees F.
Take a medium bowl and add all the dry ingredients then mix well.
Add grated butter then whisk in egg and sour cream.
Mix well using a fork and make a smooth dough.

Divide the dough into 8 wedges of ¾ inch thickness.
Place the wedges in a baking tray and drizzle sweetener on top.
Bake the wedges for 17 minutes in the preheated oven.
Serve.

Nutritional Values:
Calories 267
Total Fat 24.5 g
Saturated Fat 17.4 g
Cholesterol 153 mg
Sodium 217 mg
Total Carbs 8.4 g
Sugar 2.3 g
Fiber 1.3 g
Protein 3.1 g

Hazelnut Zucchini Bread
Preparation time: 10 minutes
Cooking time: 60 minutes
Servings: 24
Ingredients:
3 cups almond flour
1 teaspoon salt
1 teaspoon baking soda
3 teaspoons ground cinnamon
1/4 teaspoon baking powder
3 eggs
2 cups swerve
3 teaspoons vanilla extract
1 cup of vegetable oil
3 cups grated zucchini
1 cup chopped hazelnuts
How to prepare:
Start by preparing and preheating the oven at 350 degrees F.
Layer a baking pan with cooking oil or flour.
Mix all the dry bread ingredients together in a separate bowl.
Beat the wet bread ingredients together in another bowl until smooth.
Stir in flour mixture, zucchini and hazelnuts then mix well.

Spread this batter in the prepared pan
Bake them for 60 minutes approximately.
Slice and serve.

Nutritional Values:
Calories 245
Total Fat 19.9 g
Saturated Fat 4.8 g
Cholesterol 32 mg
Sodium 597 mg
Total Carbs 3.4 g
Sugar 1.9 g
Fiber 0.6 g
Protein 10.29 g

Chocolate Zucchini Bread
Preparation time: 10 minutes
Cooking time: 60 minutes
Servings: 20
Ingredients:
2 (1 ounce) squares unsweetened chocolate
3 eggs
2 cups swerve
1 cup of vegetable oil
2 cups grated zucchini
1 teaspoon vanilla extract
2 cups almond flour
1 teaspoon baking soda
1 teaspoon salt
1 teaspoon ground cinnamon
How to prepare:
Start by preparing and preheating the oven at 350 degrees F.
Layer two 9x5 inches pan with cooking oil and flour.
Add unsweetened chocolate to a glass bowl and melt in the microwave.
Mix all the dry bread ingredients together in a separate bowl.
Beat the wet bread ingredients together in another bowl until smooth.
Stir in flour mixture, zucchini, and chocolate, then mix well.
Divide the zucchini batter in the pans.

Bake them for 60 minutes approximately.
Slice and serve.

Nutritional Values:
Calories 216
Total Fat 20.9 g
Saturated Fat 8.1 g
Cholesterol 241 mg
Total Carbs 8.3 g
Sugar 1.8 g
Fiber 3.8 g
Sodium 8 mg
Protein 6 g

Strawberry Almond Bread

Preparation time: 10 minutes
Cooking time: 50 minutes
Servings: 8
Ingredients:
2 cups fresh strawberries
3 1/8 cups almond flour
2 cups swerve
1 tablespoon ground cinnamon
1 teaspoon salt
1 teaspoon baking soda
1 1/4 cups vegetable oil
4 eggs, beaten
1 1/4 cups chopped pecans
How to prepare:
Start by preparing and preheating the oven at 350 degrees F.
Layer two 9x5 inches pan with cooking oil and flour.
Mix all the dry bread ingredients together in a separate bowl.
Beat the wet bread ingredients together in another bowl until smooth.
Stir in flour mixture, strawberries and pecans, then mix well.
Divide the strawberry batter in the pans.
Bake them for 50 minutes approximately.
Slice and serve.

Nutritional Values:
Calories 301
Total Fat 26.3 g
Saturated Fat 14.8 g
Cholesterol 322 mg
Sodium 597 mg
Total Carbs 2.6 g
Fiber 0.6 g
Sugar 1.9 g
Protein 12 g

Zucchini Carrot Bread

Preparation time: 10 minutes
Cooking time: 60 minutes
Servings: 12
Ingredients:
3 eggs
1 cup of vegetable oil
2 cups swerve
1 cup grated zucchini
1 cup grated carrots
2 teaspoons vanilla extract
3 cups almond flour
3 teaspoons ground cinnamon
1 teaspoon baking soda
1/4 teaspoon baking powder
1 teaspoon salt
1/2 cup chopped walnuts
How to prepare:
Start by preparing and preheating the oven at 325 degrees F.
Layer two 8x4 inches pan with cooking oil and flour.
Mix all the dry bread ingredients together in a separate bowl.
Beat the wet bread ingredients together in another bowl until smooth.
Stir in flour mixture, carrot, and zucchini, then mix well.
Divide the zucchini batter in the pans.

Bake them for 60 minutes approximately.
Slice and serve.

Nutritional Values:
Calories 248
Total Fat 19.3 g
Saturated Fat 4.8 g
Cholesterol 32 mg
Sodium 597 mg
Total Carbs 3.1 g
Fiber 0.6 g
Sugar 1.9 g
Protein 7.9 g

Lemon Blueberry Bread
Preparation time: 10 minutes
Cooking time: 60 minutes
Servings: 12
Ingredients:
1/3 cup melted butter
1 cup swerve
3 tablespoons lemon juice
2 eggs
1 1/2 cups almond flour
1 teaspoon baking powder
1 teaspoon salt
1/2 cup almond milk
2 tablespoons grated lemon zest
1/2 cup chopped walnuts
1 cup fresh or frozen blueberries
2 tablespoons lemon juice
1/4 cup swerve
How to prepare:
Start by preparing and preheating the oven at 350 degrees F.
Layer an 8x4 inches pan with cooking oil.
Mix all the dry bread ingredients together in a separate bowl.
Beat the wet bread ingredients together in another bowl until smooth.
Stir in flour mixture, lemon zest, blueberries, and nuts, then mix well.
Divide the berries batter in the pans.
Bake them for 60 minutes approximately.
Slice and serve.

Nutritional Values:
Calories 179
Total Fat 15.7 g
Saturated Fat 8 g
Cholesterol 0 mg
Sodium 43 mg
Total Carbs 4.8 g
Sugar 3.6 g
Fiber 0.8 g
Protein 5.6 g

Chapter 4

No Carb Flatbread Recipes

Buttery flatbread
Prep Time: 10 minutes
Cooking Time: 10 minutes
Servings: 4

Ingredients:
1 cup almond flour
2 tablespoon coconut flour
2 teaspoon xanthan gum
½ teaspoon baking powder
½ teaspoon salt
1 whole egg + 1 egg white
1 tablespoon water
1 tablespoon oil for frying
1 tablespoon melted butter for slathering

How to prepare:
Start by whisking xanthan gum with flours, salt, and baking powder in a suitable bowl.
Whisk egg with egg whites in another bowl then slowly stir in flours mixture.
Stir well until smooth, then pour in tablespoon water if the dough is too thick.
Slice the dough into 4 equal parts and then roll them into ¼ inch thick rounds.

Set a large skillet over medium heat and pour in oil to heat.
Place one round in the skillet and sear for 1 minute per side.
Cook the remaining flatbreads in the skillet and arrange them in a platter.
Meanwhile, whisk butter with salt and parsley.
Drizzle this mixture over the cooked bread.
Serve warm.

Nutritional Values:
Calories 272
Total Fat 18 g
Saturated Fat 5 g
Cholesterol 6.1 mg
Sodium 3 mg
Total Carbs 4 g
Fiber 3 g
Sugar 4 g
Protein 0.4 g

Cloud Flatbread
Prep Time: 15 minutes
Cooking Time: 25 minutes
Servings: 4

Ingredients:
3 eggs
3 tablespoon coconut cream
1/2 teaspoon baking powder
sea salt black pepper
rosemary

How to prepare:
Start by preparing and preheating your oven up to 325 degrees F.
Line a suitable baking sheet with parchment sheet.
Remove the egg's yolks from whites and whisk the yolks with coconut cream in a bowl.
Whisk well with a handheld blender in the bowl until fluffy.
Now beat egg whites with baking powder in another bowl using the hand blender.
Stir in egg yolk mixture to the white's mixture and beat well.

Drop the batter dollop by dollop onto the baking sheet and spread into 4-inch circles over it.

Bake these cloud bread for 25 minutes approximately in the oven. Enjoy.

Nutritional Values:
Calories 233
Total Fat 20.2 g
Saturated Fat 4.4 g
Cholesterol 120 mg
Sodium 76 mg
Total Carbs 3.5 g
Fiber 0.9 g
Sugar 1.4 g
Protein 1.9 g

Pita Flatbreads

Preparation time: 10 minutes
Cooking time: 16 minutes
Servings: 8
Ingredients:
1 cup of warm water
1 package, 2 1/4 teaspoons active dry yeast
1 tablespoon sugar-free maple syrup
1 1/2 cups coconut flour
1 cup almond flour
1/2 teaspoon salt
canola oil for brushing
How to prepare:
Mix water with sweetener, yeast, and water in a mixing bowl.
Allow the mixed yeast to sit for 10 minutes.
Stir in salt and flour, then mix well to prepare a dough.
Knead this dough for 5 minutes or more on the working surface.
Allow this kneaded dough to rest for 2 hours.
Divide the dough into 8 equal pieces and keep them aside.
Roll each piece into a round sheet.
Place an iron skillet greased with canola oil over medium-high heat.

Spread one round dough sheet in the skillet and cook for 1 minute per side.

Serve.

Nutritional Values:
Calories 331
Total Fat 12.9 g
Saturated Fat 6.1 g
Cholesterol 10 mg
Sodium 18 mg
Total Carbs 9.1 g
Sugar 2.8 g
Fiber 0.8 g
Protein 4.4 g

Mediterranean Keto flatbread

Preparation time: 10 minutes
Cooking time: 25 minutes
Servings: 4
Ingredients:
½ cup coconut flour
1 tablespoon ground psyllium husk powder
¼ cup olive oil
1 cup boiling water
⅓ cup grated parmesan cheese
½ teaspoon of sea salt
¼ teaspoon granulated garlic
½ tablespoon black peppercorns
½ tablespoon dried rosemary
How to prepare:
Start by whisking all the dry ingredients in a suitable mixing bowl.
Stir in cheese and olive oil and mix well.
Continue adding other ingredients with constant mixing until smooth and elastic.
Spread this dough into a uniform 1/8-inch-thick sheet.
Place this bread in a baking sheet lined with parchment paper.
Bake the bread for 25 minutes approximately at 350 degrees F.

Slice and serve.

Nutritional Values:
Calories 237
Total Fat 22 g
Saturated Fat 9 g
Cholesterol 35 mg
Sodium 118 mg
Total Carbs 5 g
Sugar 1 g
Fiber 2 g
Protein 5 g

Keto Nigella Bread

Preparation time: 10 minutes
Cooking time: 15 minutes
Servings: 6
Ingredients:
Dry Ingredients
3/4 cup coconut flour
2 tablespoon psyllium husk powder
1 teaspoon xanthan gum
1 teaspoon baking powder
Generous pinch salt
1 tablespoon nigella seeds
Wet Ingredients
1 cup hot water
1/4 cup natural yogurt
2 tablespoon coconut oil melted-
Topping
2 tablespoon coconut oil, melted
handful chopped parsley
generous pinch salt
How to prepare:
Start by preparing and preheat in the oven at 356 degrees F.
Now whisk all the ingredients in a suitable bowl.
Separately whisk the wet ingredients in another bowl.

Slowly stir in flour mixture and mix well until smooth.

Divide this dough into 6 pieces then spread them into ½ cm thick sheet.

Layer 2 baking sheets with parchment sheet.

Spread the flatbread dough into the prepared baking sheets.

Drizzle sesame seeds and nigella seeds over the flatbread.

Bake these flatbreads for 15 minutes until golden brown.

Garnish with melted butter, salt, parsley, etc.

Serve.

Nutritional Values:
Calories 190
Total Fat 17.5 g
Saturated Fat 7.1 g
Cholesterol 20 mg
Sodium 28 mg
Total Carbs 5.5 g
Sugar 2.8 g
Fiber 3.8 g
Protein 3 g

Griddled flatbreads

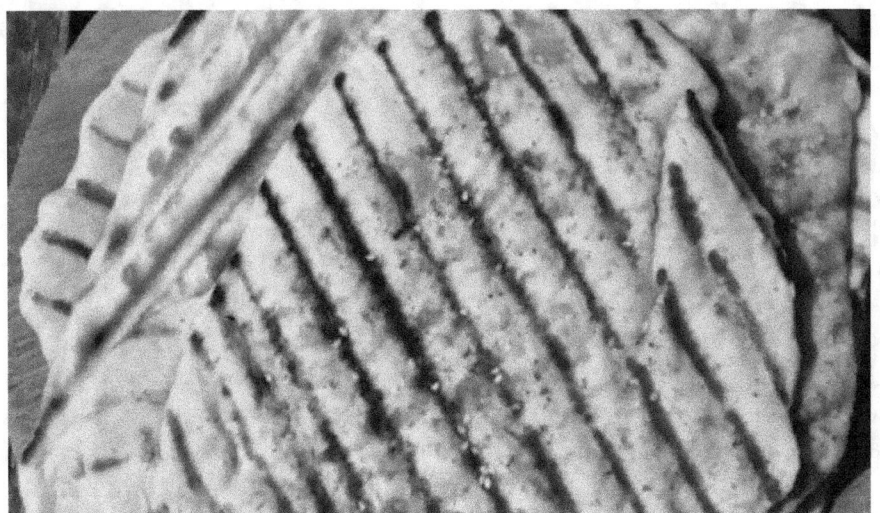

Preparation time: 10 minutes
Cooking time: 48 minutes
Servings: 8
Ingredients:
9 oz. almond meal
9 oz. almond flour
4 teaspoon sachets easy-blend yeast
1 teaspoon swerve
2 tablespoons olive oil
How to prepare:
Start by adding flours, sweetener, yeast, and a teaspoon of salt to a food processor.

Add oil and warm water then blend well for 1 minute in the processor.

Leave this dough for 1 hour in a bowl until it raised.

Blend the dough again then divide the dough into half then shape each half into a rectangle.

Cut each rectangle into eight squares of equal size.

Layer a baking tray with parchment sheet and place the squares in the baking tray.

Leave them aside for 30 minutes at room temperature.

Cook these flatbreads in a grill by cooking for 3 minutes per side.
Almond meal flatbreads

Preparation time: 10 minutes
Cooking time: 2 minutes
Servings: 8
Ingredients:
12 oz. almond meal
4 teaspoon cold-pressed rapeseed oil
How to prepare:
Start by tossing flour into a medium bowl and then add oil and 225 ml warm water.

Mix well to a form smooth dough then knead it well.

Divide the almond dough into eight balls of equal size. Roll each ball into a flatbread.

Place a nonstick skillet over medium heat then start cooking the flatbreads.

Spread one flatbread in the skillet and cook it for 1 minute per side.

Cook the remaining flatbreads following the same procedure.

Serve fresh.

Nutritional Values:
Calories 285
Total Fat 17.3 g
Saturated Fat 4.5 g
Cholesterol 175 mg
Sodium 165 mg
Total Carbs 3.5 g
Sugar 0.4 g
Fiber 0.9 g
Protein 7.2 g

Lamb Flatbread

Preparation time: 10 minutes
Cooking time: 35 minutes
Servings: 6
Ingredients:
1 teaspoon dried yeast
14 oz. almond flour
1 teaspoon salt
a little oil
For the spicy lamb topping
18 oz. lean lamb
leg meat, finely chopped (or lean mince)
1 tablespoon olive oil
1 onion, finely chopped
2 garlic cloves, finely chopped
2 teaspoon Turkish chili flakes or 1teaspoon chili flakes
2 teaspoon ground cumin
2 teaspoon ground cinnamon
4 tablespoon tomato purée
14 oz. can plum tomatoes, drained
2 small red onions, thinly sliced into half-moons
1 tablespoon pine nuts
¼ cup feta, crumbled
2 tablespoon chopped flat-leaf parsley
1 teaspoon pomegranate seeds
How to prepare:
Start by whisking yeast with 250 ml warm water in a bowl.
Allow the mixed yeast to sit for 10 minutes until foamy.
Mix this yeast mixture with flour and salt in a mixing bowl.
Once it forms a smooth dough, knead it well.
Wrap this dough in a plastic sheet for 2 hours.
Meanwhile, prepare and preheat the oven at 428 degrees F.
Place a baking sheet in the middle portion of the oven.
Sauté minced lamb with onion, and garlic for 15 minutes.
Stir in remaining spices, tomatoes, puree, and seasonings.
Mix well and stir cook the lamb for 5 minutes.

Spread the dough into a large rectangular flatbread in a greased baking sheet.

Top the bread with lamb mixture, pine nuts, feta and onions on top.

Bake the lamb pizza bread for 15 minutes until crispy.

Garnish as desired.

Serve.

Nutritional Values:
Calories 198
Total Fat 19.2 g
Saturated Fat 11.5 g
Cholesterol 123 mg
Sodium 142 mg
Total Carbs 4.5 g
Sugar 3.3 g
Fiber 0.3 g
Protein 3.4 g

Curried flatbread

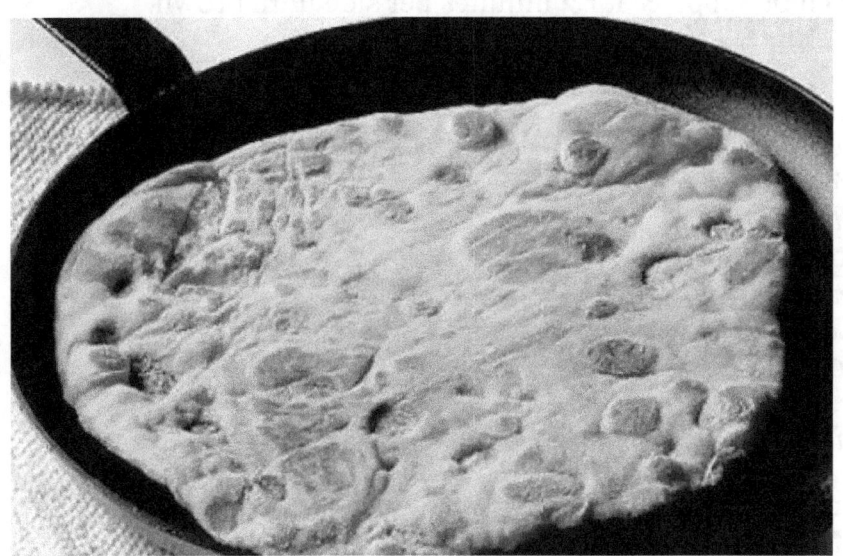

Preparation time: 10 minutes
Cooking time: 48 minutes
Servings: 8
Ingredients:
18 oz. coconut flour
2 teaspoon salt
2 tablespoon sachet fast-action yeast
3 tablespoons olive oil
1 ¼ cup water
3.5 oz. sultanas
2 oz. mild curry powder
3 tablespoon tamarind chutney
How to prepare:
Start by throwing all the ingredients in a food processor.
Blend them well until it forms a smooth dough.
Leave this dough for 1 hour at room temperature.
Spread the dough into a flatbread square.
Place the dough on a working surface.
Drizzle curry powder, sultanas and chutney over the bread dough.
Fold the dough sheet like a book and press gently.
Slice the dough into 8 pieces then place them in the baking sheet.

Place a nonstick skillet on medium heat.
Cook each bread piece for 3 minutes per side until brown.
Serve warm.

Nutritional Values:
Calories 288
Total Fat 25.3 g
Saturated Fat 6.7 g
Cholesterol 23 mg
Sodium 74 mg
Total Carbs 9.6 g
Sugar 0.1 g
Fiber 3.8 g
Protein 7.6 g

Cinnamon Flatbread
Preparation time: 10 minutes
Cooking time: 9 minutes
Servings: 8
Ingredients:
Dough Ingredients
1/3 cup coconut flour
2 tablespoon swerve confectioners
1/2 teaspoon baking powder
1/2 teaspoon cinnamon
1/8 teaspoon salt
1 1/2 cups shredded mozzarella cheese
2 tablespoon cream cheese
2 large eggs slightly beaten
2 tablespoons heavy whipping cream

Topping Ingredients
3 tablespoon butter melted
3 tablespoon swerve brown
2 1/2 tablespoon swerve confectioners
1/2 teaspoon cinnamon
1/8 teaspoon vanilla extract
How to prepare:

Start by preheating and preparing your oven at 425 degrees F.
Layer a baking tray with parchment sheet.
Whisk all the dry bread ingredients in a bowl and keep them aside.
Now melt cheese with cream cheese in a bowl by heating in the microwave for 45 seconds.
Mix well then whisk this mixture with eggs, whipping cream and dry flour mixture.
Whisk well and knead until it forms a smooth dough.
Spread this dough into a 1/3-inch-thick sheet,
Spread this dough sheet into a baking tray.
Bake this flatbread for 6 minutes approximately.

Topping Instructions
Melt butter and mix with the remaining toppings.
Spread this mixture over this bread and bake again for 2 minutes.
Slice into 8 pieces.
Serve.

Nutritional Values:
 Calories 114
  Total Fat 9.6 g
  Saturated Fat 4.5 g
  Cholesterol 10 mg
  Sodium 155 mg
  Total Carbs 3.1 g
  Sugar 1.4 g
  Fiber 1.5 g
  Protein 3.g

Sandwich Bread

Preparation time: 10 minutes
Cooking time: 10 minutes
Servings: 8
Ingredients:
1 1/2 tablespoons coconut flour
1 tablespoon coconut oil, melted
1 egg
1/8 teaspoon sea salt
1/4 teaspoon baking powder
How to prepare:
Start by preparing and preheating the oven at 350 degrees F.
Whisk all coconut flour with baking powder and sea salt in a bowl.
Stir in melted coconut oil and egg then whisk well.
Allow this batter to rest for 5 minutes.
Divide the batter into 5 inches circles on the baking sheet.
Bake the batter for 10 minutes approximately golden brown.
Serve warm and fresh.

Nutritional Values:
Calories 252
Total Fat 17.3 g
Saturated Fat 11.5 g
Cholesterol 141 mg
Sodium 153 mg
Total Carbs 7.2 g
Sugar 0.3 g
Fiber 1.4 g
Protein 5.2 g

Ingredients Flatbread

Preparation time: 10 minutes
Cooking time: 36 minutes
Servings: 6
Ingredients:
1 cup full fat natural plain yogurt
1 cup almond flour
2 teaspoons baking powder
toppings
1/2 cup butter
2-3 cloves garlic finely minced
parsley roughly chopped
1 pinch salt to taste
How to prepare:
In a large bowl whisk almond flour with baking powder.
Stir in yogurt and mix well until incorporated.
Divide this dough into 6 balls of 2 oz.
Spread each ball into an 8-inch circle.
Place a skillet over medium heat to preheat.
Add butter with garlic and salt in a bowl and heat for 30 seconds in the microwave.

Brush both sides of the dough circles with this butter mixture.
Cook them one by one in the skillet for 3 minutes per side.
Drizzle parsley on top.
Serve.

Nutritional Values:
Calories 195
Total Fat 14.3 g
Saturated Fat 10.5 g
Cholesterol 175 mg
Sodium 125 mg
Total Carbs 4.5 g
Sugar 0.5 g
Fiber 0.3 g
Protein 3.2 g

Spinach Pesto Flatbread

Preparation time: 10 minutes
Cooking time: 23 minutes
Servings: 6
Ingredients:
1 cup of almond flour
2 1/2 cups of shredded mozzarella
2 ounces of cream cheese
2 tablespoons of basil pesto
1 cup of chopped baby spinach
red pepper flakes, for topping, optional
shredded parmesan, for topping, optional
How to prepare:
Start by preparing and preheating the oven at 350 degrees F.
Layer a baking tray with parchment sheet and keep it aside.
Whisk almond flour with cream cheese and mozzarella in a bowl.
Heat this mixture in a microwave for 1 minute.
Mix well to form a smooth dough then spread this dough in the baking sheet.
Bake it for 6 minutes approximately until golden brown from top.
Now spread the spinach and red pepper flakes on top.

Bake the bread for another 16 minutes. Serve warm.

Nutritional Values:
Calories 151
Total Fat 14.7 g
Saturated Fat 1.5 g
Cholesterol 13 mg
Sodium 53 mg
Total Carbs 1.5 g
Sugar 0.3 g
Fiber 0.1 g
Protein 0.8 g

Rosemary Focaccia Bread

Preparation time: 10 minutes
Cooking time: 30 minutes
Servings: 10
Ingredients:
For the dough:
2 cups lukewarm water
1 teaspoon active dry yeast
1 tablespoon granulated swerve
5 sprigs fresh rosemary leaves, chopped
5 1/4 cups almond flour
1 tablespoon kosher salt
1 cup olive oil, divided
For the brine:
3/4 teaspoon fine sea salt
1/3 cup lukewarm water
How to prepare:
Take a large bowl and whisk water with swerve and yeast in this bowl.
Stir in 2 teaspoon rosemary, salt and half of the flour.
Mix well then add half cup olive oil along with remaining half of the flour.
Stir well to a form a dough then transfers this dough to a greased bowl.
Cover it with plastic wrap then leave for 10 hours.
Grease a rimmed baking tray with remaining half of the oil.
Spread the prepared dough in the baking tray.
Press the dough lightly using your fingers and stretch it to fit the pan.
Cover the focaccia dough with plastic wrap and leave it for 10 minutes.
Meanwhile, mix warm water with salt then pour it over the dough.
Again cover this dough and leave for 45 minutes.
Drizzle rosemary and salt over the bread.
Bake it for 30 minutes at most in the oven at 450 degrees F.

Nutritional Values:
Calories 261
Total Fat 7.1 g
Saturated Fat 13.4 g
Cholesterol 0.3 mg

Sodium 10 mg
Total Carbs 6.1 g
Sugar 2.1 g
Fiber 3.9 g
]Protein 1.8 g

Plain focaccia

Preparation time: 10 minutes
Cooking time: 20 minutes
Servings: 8
Ingredients:
1lb 2oz almond flour
2 teaspoon salt
2 sachets dried easy blend yeast
2 tablespoons olive oil
14fl oz. cold water
olive oil, for drizzling
fine sea salt
How to prepare:
Start by whisking the flour with olive oil, yeast, salt, and water.
Mix well until it forms a smooth dough.
Knead it well then place in a bowl. Wrap it with a plastic sheet.
Leave it for 2 hours.
Layer two baking trays with parchment sheets.
Divide the dough in half and spread each into the prepared baking trays.
Press the edges to set the dough in the trays.
Leave it for 1 hour.
Drizzle salt and oil over the bread.
Bake the focaccia bread for 20 minutes at 350 degrees F in a preheated oven.
Serve fresh and warm.

Nutritional Values:
Calories 139
Total Fat 4.6 g
Saturated Fat 0.5 g
Cholesterol 1.2 mg
Sodium 83 mg
Total Carbs 7.5 g
Sugar 6.3 g
Fiber 0.6 g
Protein 3.8 g

Coconut-Psyllium Flatbread

Preparation time: 10 minutes
Cooking time: 48 minutes
Servings: 16
Ingredients:
1/2 cup coconut flour
2 tablespoon psyllium seed husks
1 tablespoon olive oil
1 teaspoon baking powder
1 teaspoon salt
1 cup of warm water
How to prepare:
Start by throwing all the ingredients to a bowl.
Mix well and stir in water.
Continue mixing until it forms a smooth dough.
Knead it for 1 minute then leave it for 10 minutes.
Slice the dough into 4 equal pieces.
Spread each piece into 8 inch in diameter circle.
Place a flat pan on medium heat.
Spread one piece of dough in the pan and cook for 2-3 minutes per side until golden brown.
Cook the remaining bread in the same manner.
Serve warm and fresh.

Nutritional Values:
Calories 200
Total Fat 11.1 g
Saturated Fat 9.5 g
Cholesterol 124.2 mg
Sodium 46 mg
Total Carbs 1.1 g
Sugar 1.3 g
Fiber 0.4 g
Protein 0.4 g

Za'atar Focaccia

Preparation time: 10 minutes
Cooking time: 15 minutes
Servings: 9
Ingredients:
1 cup of warm water
2¼ teaspoons active dry yeast
1 teaspoon swerve
2¾ cups almond flour
1 teaspoon salt
8 oz. cherry tomatoes, halved
2 teaspoons Za'atar
4 tablespoons olive oil
How to prepare:
Start by whisking yeast with warm water, and sweetener in a bowl.
Mix well and leave this mixture for 10 minutes.
Meanwhile, whisk the flour with salt and Za'atar mix.
Gradually add a tablespoon of olive oil and yeast mixture with constant stirring.
Once it forms a smooth dough knead it for 5 minutes.
Now cover this dough with a plastic wrap and leave it for about 1 hour.
During this time prepare and preheat your oven at 430 degrees F.
Grease a baking tray with 1 tablespoon olive oil.
Spread the prepared dough in the baking tray and press some holes in this dough.
Drizzle the remaining 2 tablespoon oil over the dough and insert tomatoes in the wholes.
Bake this tomato bread for 15 minutes approximately until golden brown.
Slice and serve fresh.
Nutritional Values:
Calories 176
Total Fat 7.2 g
Saturated Fat 6.4 g
Cholesterol 134 mg
Sodium 8 mg
Total Carbs 2g

Sugar 1 g
Fiber 0.7 g
Protein 2.2 g

Garlic Parmesan Focaccia

Preparation time: 10 minutes
Cooking time: 87 minutes
Servings: 8
Ingredients:
GARLIC:
1 head garlic
1 teaspoon olive oil
Kosher salt
FOCACCIA:
2-1/4 cups almond flour
1-1/2 teaspoons dry instant yeast
1-1/2 teaspoons granulated swerve
1-1/2 teaspoons kosher salt
3/4 cup warm water
1/2 cup olive oil, divided
1 cup coarsely grated Parmesan-Regina
How to prepare:
Start by preparing and preheating the oven at 400 degrees F.
Place an aluminum sheet on a baking tray.
Add garlic bulb along with salt and olive oil over this foil.
Nicely wrap the foil sheet around the garlic and bake for 45 minutes.
Allow it to cool aside.
FOCACCIA:
Now whisk all the dry ingredients together in a bowl.
Continue adding water and ¾ of the oil while mixing the dough well until smooth.
Squeeze the baked garlic pulp out of its skin and add to the dough.
Knead this dough well then transfer to a bowl.
Cover this garlic dough with a kitchen towel and leave it for 2 hours.
Drizzle remaining oil in a baking tray.
Spread the garlic dough into this greased tray.
Drizzle parmesan Regina on top.
Bake the focaccia bread for 22 minutes in a preheated oven at 425 degrees F.

Nutritional Values:
Calories 193
Total Fat 10 g
Saturated Fat 13.2 g
Cholesterol 120 mg
Sodium 8 mg
Total Carbs 2.5 g
Sugar 1 g
Fiber 0.7 g
Protein 2.2 g

Chapter 5
Keto Snacks Recipes

Blueberry Scones

Prep Time: 5 minutes
Cooking Time: 25 minutes
Servings: 12

Ingredients:
2 cups almond flour
1/3 cup swerve sweetener
1/4 cup coconut flour
1 tablespoon baking powder
1/4 teaspoon salt
2 large eggs
1/4 cup heavy whipping cream
1/2 teaspoon vanilla extract
3/4 cup fresh blueberries

How to prepare:
Start by preheating your oven at 325 degrees F. Layer a baking sheet with wax paper.

Whisk almond flour with baking powder, salt, coconut flour, and sweetener in a large bowl.

Stir in eggs, vanilla and cream, mix well until fully incorporated.

Add blueberries and mix gently.

Spread this dough on a baking sheet in a 10x8 inch rectangle.

Slice the dough into 6 equal-sized square then cut each diagonally to get triangles.

Arrange these triangles in the baking sheet with 1-inch distance in between.

Bake these scones for 25 minutes until golden.

Allow them to cool then serve.

Nutritional Values:
Calories 266
Total Fat 25.7 g
Saturated Fat 1.2 g
Cholesterol 41 mg
Sodium 18 mg
Total Carbs 9.7 g
Sugar 1.2 g
Fiber 0.5 g
Protein 2.6 g

Homemade Crackers

Prep Time: 5 minutes
Cooking Time: 30 minutes
Servings: 12

Ingredients:
2 cups almond flour
1/3 cup Swerve Brown
2 teaspoon cinnamon
1 teaspoon baking powder
Pinch salt
1 large egg
2 tablespoon butter melted
1 teaspoon vanilla extract

How to prepare:
Start by preheating your oven at 300 degrees F.
Whisk almond flour, baking powder, salt, cinnamon, and sweeteners in a large bowl.
Stir in melted butter, egg, vanilla extract and molasses.
Mix well to form the dough then spread it into ¼ inch thick sheet.
Slice the sheet into 2x2 inch squares then place them in a baking sheet with wax paper.
Bake them for 30 minutes until golden. Leave them for 30 minutes until cooled.
Break the crackers and return them to the oven. Let them sit for 30 minutes.
Enjoy.

Nutritional Values:
Calories 243
Total Fat 21 g
Saturated Fat 18.2 g
Cholesterol 121 mg
Sodium 34 mg
Total Carbs 7.3 g

Sugar 0.9 g
Fiber 0.1 g
Protein 4.3 g

Chicken Sausage Balls
Prep Time: 5 minutes
Cooking Time: 25 minutes
Servings: 12

Ingredients:
Sausage Balls:
2 -14-ounce sausage, casings removed
2 cups almond flour
1 ½ cups shredded cheddar cheese
½ cup crumbled blue cheese
1 teaspoon salt
½ teaspoon pepper

Dipping Sauce:
½ teaspoon pepper
1/3 cup mayonnaise
1/3 cup almond milk, unsweetened
2 cloves garlic minced
½ teaspoon salt
1 teaspoon dill, dried
½ teaspoon parsley, dried
¼ cup crumbled bleu cheese

How to prepare:
For sausages, start by preheating your oven at 350 degrees F.
Layer two baking sheets with wax paper and keep it aside.
Mix sausage with cheddar cheese, almond flour, salt, pepper, and bleu cheese in a large bowl.
Make 1 inch balls out of this mixture and place them in the baking sheets.
Bake them for 25 minutes until golden brown.
Meanwhile, prepare the sauce by stirring all of its ingredients in a bowl.
Serve the balls with this dipping sauce.

Nutritional Values:
Calories 183
Total Fat 15 g
Saturated Fat 12.1 g
Cholesterol 11 mg
Sodium 31 mg
Total Carbs 6.2 g
Sugar 1.6 g
Fiber 0.8 g
Protein 4.5 g

Mocha Latte Fat Bomb

Preparation time: 10 minutes
Cooking time: 0minutes
Servings: 06
Ingredients:
2 medium avocados
3 scoops MCT powder
1 tablespoon organic matcha green tea powder
2 tablespoons monk fruit sweetener
1 teaspoon organic vanilla extract
3 tablespoons coconut oil
2 tablespoons coconut cream for the coating
1 tablespoon organic matcha green tea powder
1 tablespoon powdered monk fruit sweetener

How to prepare:
Blend all the ingredients in a blender.
Refrigerate the mixture for 30 minutes.
Make about 12 small balls out of this mixture.
Mix coating ingredients in a shallows bowl.
Roll the balls in this mixture to coat well.
Serve.

Nutritional Values:
Calories 272
Total Fat 18 g
Saturated Fat 5 g
Cholesterol 6.1 mg
Sodium 3 mg
Total Carbs 4 g
Fiber 3 g
Sugar 4 g
Protein 0.4 g

Matcha Fat Bombs
Preparation time: 10 minutes
Cooking time: 1 minute
Servings: 6

Ingredients:
1/2 cup raw cocoa butter
2 tablespoons coconut oil
2 tablespoons cream cheese, softened
1 scoop Perfect Keto Matcha MCT Oil Powder
1/2 teaspoon cinnamon
1/4 cup HWC

How to prepare:
Melt cocoa butter in a bowl by heating in a microwave for 30 seconds.

Blend all the ingredients, including melted butter in a bowl using an electric mixer.

Pour this matcha mixture into silicone molds and freeze for 4 hours immediately.

Remove the bombs from the molds and serve.

Nutritional Values:

Calories 188
Total Fat 6 g
Saturated Fat 1 g
Cholesterol 72 mg
Sodium 472 mg
Total Carbs 5 g
Fiber 1.6 g
Sugar 2.3 g
Protein 2.5

Blackberry Fat Bombs

Preparation time: 15 minutes
Cooking time: 0 minutes
Servings: 6
Ingredients:
1 cup coconut butter
1 cup of coconut oil
1/2 cup fresh or frozen blackberries
1/2 teaspoon stevia drops
1/4 teaspoon vanilla powder
1 tablespoon lemon juice

How to prepare:
Add coconut butter with blackberries, coconut oil in a cooking pot.
Cook until all the ingredients are mixed.
Transfer the butter mixture to a blender with all the remaining ingredients.
Blend well until smooth.
Line a 6-inch pan with parchment paper.
Pour the blackberry mixture into the pan and spread it evenly.
Refrigerate it for one hour.
Remove the pan and slice the bar into small squares.
Serve.

Nutritional Values:
Calories 225
Total Fat 12.7 g
Saturated Fat 6.1 g
Cholesterol 4 mg
Sodium 227 mg
Total Carbs 6.1 g
Fiber 1.4 g
Sugar 0.9 g
Protein 5.2 g

Cashew Fat Bombs

Preparation time: 10 minutes
Cooking time: 1 minute
Servings: 04
Ingredients:
1 cup of coconut oil
1 cup almond butter
¼ cup coconut flour
½ cup cacao powder
1 cup raw cashews

How to prepare:
Heat coconut oil in a saucepan with almond butter. Mix well.
Mix coconut flour with cocoa powder in a bowl.
Stir in butter mixture and mix well to combine.
Refrigerate for 15 minutes.
Meanwhile, coarsely chop the cashews in a food processor.
Place the cashews in a plate and set it aside.
Take the coconut flour mixture and make small balls out of it.
Roll these balls in the chopped cashews.
Refrigerate for 5 minutes then enjoy.

Nutritional Values:

Calories 232

Total Fat 16.4 g
Saturated Fat 10.1 g
Cholesterol 200 mg
Sodium 272 mg
Total Carbs 0.7 g
Fiber 0.2 g
Sugar 0 g
Protein 2.5 g

Cinnamon Granola

Preparation time: 10 minutes
Cooking time: 22 minutes
Servings: 04
Ingredients:
5 tablespoon flaxseed meal
5 tablespoon unsweetened coconut flakes
1 tablespoon chia seeds
1.5 oz. nuts
4 tablespoons sugar-free maple syrup
1 1/2 teaspoon ground cinnamon

How to prepare:
Start by throwing all the ingredients into a bowl except the cinnamon. Spread this mixture in a baking sheet then drizzle the cinnamon on top.
Bake them for 22 minutes at 350 degrees F in the oven.
Serve.

Nutritional Values:
Calories 183
Total Fat 15 g
Saturated Fat 12.1 g
Cholesterol 11 mg
Sodium 31 mg
Total Carbs 6.2 g
Sugar 1.6 g
Fiber 0.8 g
Protein 4.5 g

Psyllium Almond Bars

Preparation time: 10 minutes
Cooking time: 30 minutes
Servings: 04
Ingredients:
1 cup almonds, raw
1 tablespoon psyllium husk powder
2 tablespoon butter powder
2 tablespoon erythritol
1/2 tablespoon coconut oil
1 teaspoon ground cinnamon
1/2 teaspoon vanilla extract
20 drops liquid stevia

How to prepare:
Start by setting up the oven at 275 degrees F.
Throw all the ingredients into a food processor and blend for 1 minute.
Divide the mixture into suitable molds and bake them for 30 minutes.
Once cooled, serve.

Nutritional Values:
Calories 188
Total Fat 3 g
Saturated Fat 2.2 g
Cholesterol 101 mg
Sodium 54 mg
Total Carbs 3 g
Sugar 1.3 g
Fiber 0.6 g
Protein 5 g

Chapter 6

Keto Muffin Recipes

Blueberry Muffins

Preparation time: 10 minutes
Cooking time: 20 minutes
Servings: 12
Ingredients:
12 ½ oz. almond flour
1 teaspoon baking soda
2 teaspoon baking powder
Heavy pinch salt
1 cup swerve
½ cup of vegetable oil
1 egg
1 cup yogurt
1 ½ cups fresh blueberries
Vegetable spray, for the muffin tins

How to prepare:
Start by preparing and preheating the oven at 380 degrees F.
Layer muffin tray with cooking oil and keep it aside.
Mix all the dry ingredients together in a separate bowl.
Beat the wet ingredients together in another bowl until smooth.
Stir in flour mixture, and berries, then mix well.
Divide the berries batter in the muffin cups.
Bake them for 20 minutes approximately.
Slice and serve.

Nutritional Values:
Calories 197
Total Fat 19.2 g
Saturated Fat 10.1 g
Cholesterol 11 mg
Sodium 78 mg
Total Carbs 7.3 g
Sugar 1.2 g
Fiber 0.8 g
Protein 4.2 g

Avocado Muffins

Preparation time: 10 minutes
Cooking time: 25 minutes
Servings: 8
Ingredients:
2 ½ cups unbleached almond flour
½ teaspoon baking soda
¾ cup dark brown swerve
¼ teaspoon ground cinnamon
2 cups avocado mash
½ cup of vegetable oil
½ cup almond milk
2 large eggs, at room temperature
⅛ teaspoon fine salt
½ teaspoon vanilla extract
¾ cup chopped walnuts
How to prepare:
Start by preparing and preheating the oven at 380 degrees F.
Layer muffin tray with cooking oil and keep it aside.
Mix all the dry ingredients together in a separate bowl.
Beat the wet ingredients together in another bowl until smooth.
Stir in flour mixture, and nuts then mix well.
Divide the avocado muffin batter into the muffin cups.
Bake them for 25 minutes approximately.
Slice and serve.

Nutritional Values:
Calories 213
Total Fat 19 g
Saturated Fat 15.2 g
Cholesterol 13 mg
Sodium 52 mg
Total Carbs 5.5 g
Sugar 1.3 g
Fiber 0.5 g
Protein 6.1 g

Hazelnut Avocado Muffins

Preparation time: 10 minutes
Cooking time: 25 minutes
Servings: 12
Ingredients:
1 ½ cups avocado, mash
¾ cup granulated Swerve
½ cup hazelnut butter, melted
2 large eggs
1 teaspoon vanilla extract
2 cups almond flour
½ cup of cocoa powder
2 teaspoon baking powder
½ teaspoon baking soda
½ teaspoon salt
1 cup of sugar-free chocolate chips
How to prepare:
Start by preparing and preheating the oven at 380 degrees F.
Layer muffin tray with cooking oil and keep it aside.
Mix all the dry ingredients together in a separate bowl.
Beat the wet ingredients together in another bowl until smooth.
Stir in flour mixture, then mix well.
Divide the hazelnut batter into the muffin cups.
Bake them for 25 minutes approximately.
Serve.

Nutritional Values:
Calories 117
Total Fat 21.2 g
Saturated Fat 10.4 g
Cholesterol 19.7 mg
Sodium 104 mg
Total Carbs 7.3 g
Sugar 3.4 g
Fiber 2 g
Protein 8.1 g

Avocado Crunch Muffins

Preparation time: 10 minutes
Cooking time: 25 minutes
Servings: 12
Ingredients:
3 cups almond flour
2 cups swerve
2 teaspoon baking powder
1 teaspoon baking soda
½ teaspoon salt
½ lb.(s) unsalted butter, melted and cooled
2 extra-large eggs
¾ cup almond milk
2 teaspoons pure vanilla extract
2 cup avocado, mashed
1 cup walnuts, small-diced
1 cup granola
1 cup sweetened, shredded coconut
Dried banana chips, granola, or shredded coconut
How to prepare:
Mix walnuts with coconut and granola in a bowl and keep it aside.
Start by preparing and preheating the oven at 350 degrees F.
Layer muffin tray with cooking oil and keep it aside.
Mix all the dry ingredients together in a separate bowl.
Beat the wet ingredients together in another bowl until smooth.
Stir in flour mixture, then mix well.
Divide the prepared batter into the muffin cups.
Top each muffin cup with granola mixture.
Bake them for 25 minutes approximately.
Serve.

Nutritional Values:
Calories 113
Total Fat 9 g
Saturated Fat 0.2 g
Cholesterol 1.7 mg
Sodium 134 mg

Total Carbs 6.5 g
Sugar 1.8 g
Fiber 0.7 g
Protein 7.5 g

Pumpkin Chocolate Chip Muffins

Preparation time: 10 minutes
Cooking time: 30 minutes
Servings: 12
Ingredients:
1/2 cup coconut flour
2 teaspoon baking powder
1/4 teaspoon sea salt
2 teaspoon cinnamon
1 1/2 teaspoon ground ginger
1/2 teaspoon nutmeg
1/4 teaspoon ground cloves
1 1/2 cups pumpkin puree
2/3 cup coconut sugar
1/2 cup coconut oil, melted
6 eggs
1 teaspoon vanilla extract
1 cup mini sugar-free chocolate chips
How to prepare:
Start by preparing and preheating the oven at 375 degrees F.
Layer muffin tray with cooking oil and keep it aside.
Mix all the dry ingredients together in a separate bowl.
Beat the wet ingredients together in another bowl until smooth.
Stir in flour mixture, and chocolate chips then mix well.
Divide the pumpkin batter into the muffin cups.
Bake them for 30 minutes approximately.
Serve.

Nutritional Values:
Calories 183
Total Fat 15 g
Saturated Fat 12.1 g
Cholesterol 11 mg
Sodium 31 mg
Total Carbs 6.2 g
Sugar 1.6 g
Fiber 0.8 g
Protein 4.5 g

Vegan Blueberry Muffins

Preparation time: 10 minutes
Cooking time: 20 minutes
Servings: 12
Ingredients:
Cooking spray
2 cups almond flour
2 teaspoon baking powder
½ teaspoon kosher salt
⅔ cup packed light brown swerve
½ cup of soy milk yogurt
⅓ cup unsweetened almond milk
⅓ cup of vegetable oil
1 teaspoon pure vanilla extract
2 cups fresh or frozen blueberries
2 tablespoon swerve

How to prepare:
Start by preparing and preheating the oven at 350 degrees F.
Layer muffin tray with cooking oil and keep it aside.
Mix all the dry ingredients together in a separate bowl.
Beat the wet ingredients together in another bowl until smooth.

Stir in flour mixture, and berries then mix well. Divide the berries batter in the muffin cups. Bake them for 20 minutes approximately. Serve.

Nutritional Values:
Calories 153
Total Fat 13 g
Saturated Fat 9.2 g
Cholesterol 6.5 mg
Sodium 81 mg
Total Carbs 4.5 g
Sugar 1.4 g
Fiber 0.4 g
Protein 5.8 g

Crumbly Coffee Muffins

Preparation time: 10 minutes
Cooking time: 35 minutes
Servings: 12
Ingredients:
Crumb
1/2 cup almond flour
3 tablespoon Swerve Brown
2 tablespoon coconut flour
3/4 teaspoon cinnamon
1/4 cup butter melted
Muffins
2 cups almond flour
1/3 cup Swerve Sweetener
1/4 cup unflavored whey protein powder
3 tablespoon coconut flour
1 tablespoon baking powder
1/2 teaspoon cinnamon
1/4 teaspoon salt
1/2 cup butter, melted
4 large eggs

1/2 cup unsweetened almond milk
1/2 teaspoon vanilla extract
How to prepare:
Start by whisking all the ingredients for crumb topping in a bowl and keep it aside.
Now, prepare and preheat your oven at 325 degrees F.
Layer a muffin tray with muffin cups.
Add all the dry ingredients to a large bowl and mix well.
Start stirring in other ingredients and mix well until smooth.
Divide this batter in the lined muffin tray and allow it to set.
Drizzle the crumb mixture over the batter then bake for 35 minutes.
Allow the muffins to cool then serve.

Nutritional Values:
Calories 254
Total Fat 09 g
Saturated Fat 10.1 g
Cholesterol 13 mg
Sodium 179 mg
Total Carbs 7.5 g
Sugar 1.2 g
Fiber 0.8 g
Protein 7.5 g

Morning Cranberry Muffins

Preparation time: 10 minutes
Cooking time: 30 minutes
Servings: 12
Ingredients:
1 cup cranberries, chopped
1 cup swerve
1 ½ cups almond flour
1 pinch ground cinnamon
½ teaspoon baking soda
¼ teaspoon ground nutmeg
1 teaspoon salt
2 large eggs
¼ cup canola oil
1 lemon, zested
½ pt. blueberries
1 cup chopped walnuts
How to prepare:
Start by preparing and preheating the oven at 350 degrees F.
Layer muffin tray with cooking oil and keep it aside.
Mix cranberry with 2 tablespoon sweetener in a small bowl and leave it for 15 minutes. Then drain these berries.
Mix all the dry ingredients together in a separate bowl.
Beat the wet ingredients together in another bowl until smooth.
Stir in flour mixture, berries and walnuts then mix well.
Divide the berries batter in the muffin cups.
Bake them for 30 minutes approximately.
Serve.
Nutritional Values:
Calories 290
Total Fat 21.5 g
Saturated Fat 15.2 g
Cholesterol 12.1 mg
Sodium 9 mg
Total Carbs 6.5 g
Sugar 1.2 g
Fiber 0.4 g

Protein 6.2 g

Strawberry Muffins

Preparation time: 10 minutes
Cooking time: 25 minutes
Servings: 12
Ingredients:
3 cups almond flour
1 tablespoon baking powder
½ teaspoon baking soda
½ teaspoon kosher salt
1 ½ tablespoon ground cinnamon
1 ¼ cups almond milk
2 extra-large eggs, lightly beaten
½ lb. unsalted butter, melted
2 cups diced fresh strawberries
1 ½ cups swerve

How to prepare:
Start by preparing and preheating the oven at 375 degrees F.
Layer muffin tray with cooking oil and keep it aside.
Mix all the dry ingredients together in a separate bowl.
Beat the wet ingredients together in another bowl until smooth.
Stir in flour mixture, and berries then mix well.
Divide the berries batter in the muffin cups.
Bake them for 25 minutes approximately.
Serve.

Nutritional Values:

Calories 214
Total Fat 19 g
Saturated Fat 5.8 g
Cholesterol 15 mg
Sodium 123 mg
Total Carbs 6.5 g
Sugar 1.9 g

Sunflower-Butter Muffins

Preparation time: 10 minutes
Cooking time: 18 minutes
Servings: 12
Ingredients:
Cooking spray, for the paper liners
½ cup dried cranberries
1 ¼ cups almond flour
½ cup flaxseed meal
2 teaspoon baking powder
1 teaspoon kosher salt
¼ teaspoon baking soda
½ cup sugar-free chocolate chips
⅔ cup packed light brown swerve
½ cup sunflower butter
¾ cup almond milk
2 Tablespoon vegetable oil
1 large egg
How to prepare:
Start by preparing and preheating the oven at 350 degrees F.
Layer a 24 muffin tray with cooking oil and keep it aside.
Mix all the dry ingredients together in a separate bowl.
Beat the wet ingredients together in another bowl until smooth.
Stir in flour mixture, and cranberries then mix well.
Divide the cranberries batter into the muffin cups.
Bake them for 18 minutes approximately.
Serve.

Nutritional Values:
Calories 282
Total Fat 25.1 g
Saturated Fat 8.8 g
Cholesterol 100 mg
Sodium 117 mg
Total Carbs 9.4 g
Sugar 0.7 g
Fiber 3.2 g

Cheesecake Blueberry Muffin

Preparation time: 10 minutes
Cooking time: 16 minutes
Servings: 12
Ingredients:
Cheesecake Filling
4 oz. cream cheese
¼ cup sour cream
3 tablespoon granulated Swerve
Batter
Nonstick cooking spray
1 ¾ cups almond flour
½ cup almond meal
¾ cup granulated Swerve
2 teaspoon baking powder
½ teaspoon fine salt
½ cup almond milk
½ cup of vegetable oil
1 teaspoon pure vanilla extract
2 large eggs
¾ cup blueberries
How to prepare:
Start by preparing and preheating the oven at 375 degrees F.

Layer muffin tray with cooking oil and keep it aside.

Prepare the cream cheese filling by whisking all of its ingredients.

Add this filling to a plastic piping bag and refrigerate until batter is prepared.

Batter:

Mix all the dry ingredients together in a separate bowl.

Beat the wet ingredients together in another bowl until smooth.

Stir in flour mixture, then mix well.

Divide the cheesecake batter into the muffin cups and top each with cream filling.

Bake them for 16 minutes approximately.

Serve.

Nutritional Values:
Calories 331
Total Fat 38.5 g
Saturated Fat 19.2 g
Cholesterol 141 mg
Sodium 283 mg
Total Carbs 9.2 g
Sugar 3 g
Fiber 1 g
Protein 2.1 g

Chocolate Zucchini Muffins

Preparation time: 10 minutes
Cooking time: 17 minutes
Servings: 12
Ingredients:
1 cup almond flour
¾ cup swerve
⅓ cup of cocoa powder
1 teaspoon cinnamon
1 teaspoon baking soda
½ teaspoon salt
½ cup Silk, any flavor except Light
2 teaspoon vinegar
¼ cup of vegetable oil
1 egg, beaten
1 teaspoon vanilla
¾ cup grated zucchini
½ cup boiling water
½ cup of sugar-free chocolate chips
How to prepare:
Start by preparing and preheating the oven at 350 degrees F.
Layer muffin tray with cooking oil and keep it aside.
Mix all the dry ingredients together in a separate bowl.
Beat the wet ingredients together in another bowl until smooth.
Stir in flour mixture, and zucchini, then mix well.
Divide the zucchini batter into the muffin cups.
Drizzle chocolate chips over the muffin batter.
Bake them for 17 minutes approximately.
Serve.

Carrot and Zucchini Muffins

Preparation time: 10 minutes
Cooking time: 15 minutes
Servings: 24
Ingredients:
Muffins
1 cup almond flour
¼ cup coconut flour
¼ teaspoon fine sea salt
1 teaspoon baking powder
½ teaspoon baking soda
2 teaspoon ground cinnamon
⅓ cup grapeseed oil
⅓ cup sugar-free maple syrup
1 large egg, at room temperature
½ cup grated carrots
½ cup grated zucchini
½ cup raisins
Frosting
1 cup whipped cream cheese
1 ½ tablespoon sugar-free maple syrup
How to prepare:
Start by preparing and preheating the oven at 350 degrees F.
Layer muffin tray with cooking oil and keep it aside.
Mix all the dry ingredients together in a separate bowl.
Beat the wet ingredients together in another bowl until smooth.
Stir in flour mixture, carrots and zucchini then mix well.
Divide the carrots batter into the muffin cups.
Bake them for 15 minutes approximately.
Serve.

Frosting:
Prepare the muffin frosting in a mixer until smooth.
Top the baked muffin with this frosting.
Serve.

Nutritional Values:
Calories 259
Total Fat 34 g
Saturated Fat 10.3 g
Cholesterol 112 mg
Sodium 92 mg
Total Carbs 8.5 g
Sugar 2 g
Fiber 1.3 g
Protein 7.5 g

Blueberry-Carrot Muffins

Preparation time: 10 minutes
Cooking time: 24 minutes
Servings: 12
Ingredients:
Cooking spray
1 ½ cups blueberries
2 cups almond flour
2 teaspoon baking powder
1 teaspoon ground cinnamon
½ teaspoon fine salt
½ cup almond milk
½ cup melted coconut oil
½ cup brown swerve
2 medium carrots, shredded and squeezed dried
2 large eggs
1 teaspoon finely grated lemon zest
1 teaspoon pure vanilla extract
1 tablespoon swerve

How to prepare:
Start by preparing and preheating the oven at 350 degrees F.
Layer a 12 cup-muffin tray with cooking oil and keep it aside.
Mix all the dry ingredients together in a separate bowl.
Beat the wet ingredients together in another bowl until smooth.
Stir in flour mixture, and half of the berries then mix well.

Divide the berries batter in the muffin cups.
Top the muffin batter with remaining berries and sweetener.
Bake them for 24 minutes approximately.
Serve.

Nutritional Values:
Calories 255
Total Fat 23.4 g
Saturated Fat 11.7 g
Cholesterol 135 mg
Sodium 112 mg
Total Carbs 2.5 g
Sugar 12.5 g
Fiber 1 g
Protein 7.9 g

Chocolate Chip Muffins

Preparation time: 10 minutes
Cooking time: 25 minutes
Servings: 12
Ingredients:
1 cup flaxseed meal
1 ½ cups almond flour
½ cup coconut flour
2 teaspoon baking powder
½ teaspoon baking soda
¾ teaspoon of sea salt
1 teaspoon cinnamon
⅔ cup swerve
3 tablespoons avocado oil
1 cup unsweetened applesauce
1 teaspoon vanilla extract
1 cup plain kefir or almond milk
1 egg, beaten
⅔ cup dried blueberries
How to prepare:
Start by preparing and preheating the oven at 375 degrees F. Layer a 12 cup- muffin tray with cooking oil and keep it aside.

Mix all the dry ingredients together in a separate bowl.
Beat the wet ingredients together in another bowl until smooth.
Stir in flour mixture, and chocolate chips then mix well.
Divide the chocolate chips batter into the muffin cups.
Bake them for 25 minutes approximately.
Serve.

Nutritional Values:
Calories 251
Total Fat 24.5 g
Saturated Fat 14.7 g
Cholesterol 165 mg
Sodium 142 mg
Total Carbs 4.3 g
Sugar 0.5 g
Fiber 1 g
Protein 5.9 g

Pumpkin Carrot Muffins

Preparation time: 10 minutes
Cooking time: 25 minutes
Servings: 24
Ingredients:
Muffins
½ cup unsalted butter, room temperature
½ cup swerve
½ cup brown swerve
2 large eggs at room temperature
1 cup pure pumpkin puree
½ cup sour cream
1 teaspoon pure vanilla extract
2 cup almond flour
1 teaspoon baking powder
1 teaspoon baking soda
1 teaspoon salt
½ teaspoon ground cinnamon
½ teaspoon ground ginger
1 cup finely grated carrot
Frosting
¼ cup 1 tablespoon almond milk
½ cup unsalted butter, room temperature
Swerve, sifted (3-4 cups)
1 teaspoon vanilla bean paste
1 teaspoon pure vanilla extract
How to prepare:
Start by preparing and preheating the oven at 350 degrees F.
Layer a 24 cup- muffin tray with cooking oil and keep it aside.
Mix all the dry ingredients together in a separate bowl.
Beat the wet ingredients together in another bowl until smooth.
Stir in flour mixture, then mix well.
Divide the pumpkin batter into the muffin cups.
Bake them for 25 minutes approximately.
Meanwhile, prepare the frosting by beating its ingredients in a bowl.
Divide the frosting over the baked muffins.
Serve.

Nutritional Values:
Calories 165
Total Fat 14 g
Saturated Fat 7 g
Cholesterol 632 mg
Sodium 497 mg
Total Carbs 6 g
Fiber 3 g
Sugar 1 g
Protein 5 g

Blueberry Mini Muffins

Preparation time: 10 minutes
Cooking time: 24 minutes
Servings: 12
Ingredients:
2 cup almond flour
2 teaspoon baking powder
½ teaspoon salt
2 cup organic blueberries
½ cup of vegetable oil
½ cup of soy milk
½ cup sugar-free maple syrup
¼ cup agave nectar
How to prepare:
Start by preparing and preheating the oven at 375 degrees F.
Layer mini muffin tray with cooking oil and keep it aside.
Mix all the dry ingredients together in a separate bowl.
Beat the wet ingredients together in another bowl until smooth.
Stir in flour mixture, and berries then mix well.
Divide the berries batter in the muffin cups.
Bake them for 20 minutes approximately.
Serve.

Nutritional Values:

Calories 113
Total Fat 8.4 g
Saturated Fat 12.1 g
Cholesterol 27 mg
Sodium 39 mg
Total Carbs 9.2 g
Sugar 3.1 g
Fiber 4.6 g
Protein 8.1 g

Carrot, and Chocolate Chip Muffins

Preparation time: 10 minutes
Cooking time: 20 minutes
Servings: 12
Ingredients:
½ cup granulated Swerve
½ cup plain yogurt
⅓ cup canola oil
2 large eggs
1 1/2 cup carrot, grated
1 teaspoon vanilla
2 cups almond flour
1 teaspoon baking powder
½ teaspoon baking soda
½ teaspoon salt
2 tablespoon flax seeds
¼ cup flaxseed meal
1 cup of sugar-free chocolate chips

How to prepare:
Start by preparing and preheating the oven at 375 degrees F.
Layer a 12 cup muffin tray with cooking oil and keep it aside.
Melt chocolate in a bowl by heating in a microwave and keep it warm.
Mix all the dry ingredients together in a separate bowl.

Beat the wet ingredients together in another bowl until smooth.
Stir in flour mixture, then mix well.
Divide the batter into the muffin cups.
Bake them for 20 minutes approximately.
Drizzle chocolate over each muffin.
Let it stay for 15 minutes.
Serve.

Nutritional Values:
Calories 158
Total Fat 15.2 g
Saturated Fat 5.2 g
Cholesterol 269 mg
Sodium 178 mg
Total Carbs 7.4 g
Sugar 1.1 g
Fiber 3.5 g
Protein 5.5 g

Bacon Caramel Scuffins

Preparation time: 10 minutes
Cooking time: 15 minutes
Servings: 24
Ingredients:
Nonstick cooking spray, for muffin tin
6 slices Applewood-smoked bacon
1 ½ cups almond flour
1 teaspoon baking powder
⅛ teaspoon kosher salt
1 stick (8 tablespoons) unsalted butter, softened
½ cup light brown swerve
1 large egg
½ teaspoon vanilla extract
½ cup half-and-half
Topping
6 sugar-free caramel sauce
½ cup clotted cream
How to prepare:
Start by preparing and preheating the oven at 350 degrees F.
Layer a 24 cups muffin tray with cooking oil and keep it aside.
Spread the bacon in a baking sheet then bake for 20 minutes until crispy.
Chop the crispy bacon into small crumbs.
Mix all the dry ingredients together in a separate bowl.
Beat the wet ingredients together in another bowl until smooth.
Stir in flour mixture, then mix well.
Fold in chopped bacon then divide the batter into the muffin cups.
Bake them for 15 minutes approximately.
During this time mix caramel sauce with clotted cream in a bowl.
Top the muffins with this cream mixture.
Serve.

Nutritional Values:
Calories 248
Total Fat 19.3 g
Saturated Fat 4.8 g

Cholesterol 32 mg
Sodium 597 mg
Total Carbs 3.1 g
Fiber 0.6 g
Sugar 1.9 g
Protein 7.9 g

Sunshine Muffins

Preparation time: 10 minutes
Cooking time: 20 minutes
Servings: 8
Ingredients:
Gluten-Free Flour Mix
4 cup almond flour
1 ⅓ cup coconut flour
⅔ cup flaxseed meal
3 tablespoon xanthan gum
Muffins
3 cup Gluten-Free Flour Mix
1 tablespoon baking powder
¼ cup powdered almond milk
2 teaspoons freshly grated nutmeg
½ cup melted butter
1 cup brown swerve
1 tablespoon vanilla
1 ½ cup almond milk
4 tablespoon ground flax seed
¾ cup of water
½ cup dried apricots, chopped
½ cup sunflower seeds

Frosting & Topping
½ cup softened butter
2 cup confectioners' swerve
juice and zest of 1 lemon
½ cup toasted coconut

How to prepare:
Start by preparing and preheating the oven at 350 degrees F.
Layer muffin tray with cooking oil and keep it aside.
Mix all the dry ingredients together in a separate bowl.
Beat the wet ingredients together in another bowl until well incorporated.
Stir in flour mixture, then mix well.
Divide the flaxseed batter into the muffin cups.

Bake them for 20 minutes approximately.
Whisk all the ingredients for frosting in a bowl.
Spread this mixture over the muffins.
Serve.

Nutritional Values:
Calories 301
Total Fat 26.3 g
Saturated Fat 14.8 g
Cholesterol 322 mg
Sodium 597 mg
Total Carbs 2.6 g
Fiber 0.6 g
Sugar 1.9 g
Protein 12 g

Zucchini & Carrot Muffins

Preparation time: 10 minutes
Cooking time: 25 minutes
Servings: 12
Ingredients:
2 cups almond flour
¾ cup brown swerve
½ cup coconut flour
¼ cup ground flaxseed
¼ cup unsalted raw pumpkin seeds
2 tablespoons natural wheat germ
2 teaspoon baking powder
2 teaspoon cinnamon
1 cup almond milk
½ cup canola oil
2 Omega-3 eggs
1 cup finely grated zucchini
2 cups finely grated carrot
How to prepare:
Start by preparing and preheating the oven at 375 degrees F.
Layer muffin tray with cooking oil and keep it aside.
Mix all the dry ingredients together in a separate bowl.
Beat the wet ingredients together in another bowl until smooth.
Stir in flour mixture, then mix well.
Divide the zucchini batter into the muffin cups.
Bake them for 25 minutes approximately.
Serve.

Nutritional Values:
Calories 282
Total Fat 25.1 g
Saturated Fat 8.8 g
Cholesterol 100 mg
Sodium 117 mg
Total Carbs 9.4 g
Sugar 0.7 g
Fiber 3.2 g

Healthy Carrot Muffins

Preparation time: 10 minutes
Cooking time: 30 minutes
Servings: 12
Ingredients:
¾ cup almond flour
½ cup coconut flour
⅔ cup brown swerve
2 teaspoon ground cinnamon
1 teaspoon baking powder
½ teaspoon baking soda
1 pinch fine salt
2 large eggs
⅓ cup of vegetable oil
1 tablespoon pure vanilla extract
4 medium carrots, grated
½ cup canned crushed pineapple, drained
How to prepare:
Start by preparing and preheating the oven at 350 degrees F.
Layer muffin tray with cooking oil and keep it aside.
Mix all the dry ingredients together in a separate bowl.
Beat the wet ingredients together in another bowl until smooth.

Stir in flour mixture, and carrots then mix well.
Divide the carrot batter into the muffin cups.
Bake them for 30 minutes approximately.
Serve.

Nutritional Values:
Calories 245
Total Fat 19.9 g
Saturated Fat 4.8 g
Cholesterol 32 mg
Sodium 597 mg
Total Carbs 3.4 g
Sugar 1.9 g
Fiber 0.6 g
Protein 10.9 g

Chapter 7

Keto Buns Recipes

Breakfast Buns
Preparation time: 10 minutes
Cooking time: 15 minutes
Servings: 12
Ingredients:
5 cups almond flour
2 (.25 ounce) packages dry yeast
1 cup almond milk
3/4 cup water
1/2 cup vegetable oil
1/4 cup swerve
1 teaspoon salt
How to prepare:
Start by preparing and preheating oven at 400 degrees F.
First, whisk all the dry buns ingredients in a mixing bowl.
Beat the remaining wet ingredients in another bowl until foamy.
Gradually add the dry flour mixture with constant mixing.
Mix and knead this dough well to form a soft and smooth dough.
Divide the prepared dough into 12 pieces and roll them slightly.
Place the buns in a greased baking sheet and flatten them slightly.
Bake the buns for 15 minutes approximately until done.
Serve warm and fresh.

Cinnamon buns

Preparation time: 10 minutes
Cooking time: 12 minutes
Servings: 12
Ingredients:
For the cinnamon bun dough
3½oz unsalted butter
7fl oz. almond milk
1 teaspoon salt
9oz almond flour, plus extra for dusting
9oz coconut flour
1½ teaspoon fast-action yeast
1 teaspoon ground cardamom
4 tablespoon swerve
2 free-range eggs
olive oil, for greasing
For the filling and topping
2½oz unsalted butter softened
Topping
3½oz swerve
2 tablespoon cinnamon
1 free-range egg, beaten
How to prepare:
Start by preparing and preheating oven at 400 degrees F.
First, whisk all the dry buns ingredients in a mixing bowl.
Beat the remaining wet ingredients in another bowl until foamy.
Gradually add the dry flour mixture with constant mixing.
Mix and knead this dough well to form a soft and smooth dough.
Cover the dough with plastic wrap and leave for 15 minutes.
Divide the prepared dough into medium-sized 12 buns.
Place the buns in a greased baking sheet and flatten them slightly.
Whisk egg well in a bowl and brush over the buns.
Mix cinnamon with sweetener in a bowl and drizzle over the buns.
Bake the buns for 12 minutes approximately until done.
Serve warm and fresh.

Nutritional Values:
Calories 207
Total Fat 19 g
Saturated Fat 14 g
Cholesterol 111 mg
Sodium 122 mg
Total Carbs 7 g
Sugar 1 g
Fiber 3 g
Protein 6 g

Chocolate and cherry buns

Preparation time: 10 minutes
Cooking time: 25 minutes
Servings: 12
Ingredients:
For the dough
9fl oz. almond milk
2½oz butter
1lb 2oz almond flour
¼ oz. instant yeast
2½oz brown swerve
pinch salt
1 free-range egg
dash oil, for greasing your hands and the work surface
For the filling
3½oz butter softened
2fl oz. sugar-free maple syrup
1oz brown swerve
1 teaspoon ground cinnamon
1 teaspoon ground mixed spice
pinch salt
3½oz glacé cherries halved
3½oz sugar-free chocolate chips
To bake
1 free-range egg
2 tablespoon swerve
For the glaze (optional)
7oz icing swerve
1-2 tablespoon boiled water
How to prepare:
Start by preparing and preheating oven at 400 degrees F.
First, whisk all the dry bun ingredients in a mixing bowl.
Beat the remaining wet ingredients in another bowl until foamy.
Gradually add the dry flour mixture with constant mixing.
Mix and knead this dough well to form a soft and smooth dough.
Cover the dough with plastic wrap and leave for 15 minutes.
Divide the prepared dough into medium-sized 12 buns.

Place the buns in a greased baking sheet and flatten them slightly.
Whisk an egg well in a bowl and brush over the buns.
Drizzle sweetener over the buns.
Bake the buns for 25 minutes approximately until done.
Meanwhile, prepare the frosting by heating its ingredient in a saucepan for 2 minutes.
Drizzle this frosting over the baked buns.
Serve warm and fresh.

Nutritional Values:
Calories 255
Total Fat 23.4 g
Saturated Fat 11.7 g
Cholesterol 135 mg
Sodium 112 mg
Total Carbs 2.5 g
Sugar 12.5 g
Fiber 1 g
Protein 7.9 g

Chelsea buns

Preparation time: 10 minutes
Cooking time: 25 minutes
Servings: 10
Ingredients:
1lb 2oz almond flour
1 teaspoon salt
¼ oz. sachet fast-acting yeast
10fl oz. almond milk
1½oz unsalted butter
1 free-range egg
vegetable oil, for greasing
For the filling
1oz unsalted butter, melted
1 orange, zest only, grated
2½oz soft brown swerve
2 teaspoon ground cinnamon
3½oz dried cranberries
3½oz sultanas
3½oz dried apricots, chopped
To finish
1 heaped tablespoon apricot jam
7oz icing swerve, sifted
1 orange, zest only, grated

How to prepare:
Start by preparing and preheating oven at 400 degrees F.
First, whisk all the dry bun ingredients in a mixing bowl.
Beat the remaining wet ingredients in another bowl until foamy.
Gradually add the dry flour mixture with constant mixing.
Mix and knead well to form a soft and smooth dough.
Cover the dough with plastic wrap and leave for 15 minutes.
Divide the prepared dough into medium-sized 12 buns.
Place the buns in a greased baking sheet and flatten them slightly.
Bake the buns for 25 minutes approximately until done.
Meanwhile, prepare the frosting by heating its ingredient in a saucepan for 2 minutes.
Drizzle this frosting over the baked buns.

Serve warm and fresh.

Nutritional Values:
Calories 251
Total Fat 24.5 g
Saturated Fat 14.7 g
Cholesterol 165 mg
Sodium 142 mg
Total Carbs 4.3 g
Sugar 0.5 g
Fiber 1 g
Protein 5.9 g

Vegan Soya Buns

Preparation time: 10 minutes
Cooking time: 30 minutes
Servings: 9
Ingredients:
bun dough
1lb 1oz almond flour
1oz xanthan gum
¼ oz. sachet fast-action yeast
1¾oz swerve
½ teaspoon ground cardamom
½ teaspoon salt
11fl oz. soya milk
2½oz dairy-free margarine
For the caramel sauce
3 oz. dairy-free margarine
3 tablespoons soft light brown swerve
pinch of salt
How to prepare:

Start by preparing and preheating oven at 400 degrees F.
First, whisk all the dry bun ingredients in a mixing bowl.
Beat the remaining wet ingredients in another bowl until foamy.
Gradually add the dry flour mixture with constant mixing.
Mix and knead well to form a soft and smooth dough.
Cover the dough with a plastic sheet.
c wrap and leave for 15 minutes.
Divide the prepared dough into medium-sized 12 buns.
Place the buns in a greased baking sheet and flatten them slightly.
Whisk egg in a bowl and brush over the buns.
Drizzle sweetener over the buns.
Bake the buns for 30 minutes approximately until done.
Meanwhile, prepare the caramel sauce by heating its ingredient in a saucepan for 2 minutes.
Drizzle this sauce over the baked buns.
Serve warm and fresh.

Nutritional Values:
Calories 173
Total Fat 16.2 g
Saturated Fat 9.8 g
Cholesterol 100 mg
Sodium 42 mg
Total Carbs 9.4 g
Fiber 1 g
Sugar 0.2 g
Protein 3.3 g

Burger Buns

Preparation time: 10 minutes
Cooking time: 18 minutes
Servings: 8
Ingredients:
1 cup lukewarm water
2 tablespoons butter
1 large egg
3 1/2 cups unbleached almond flour
1/4 cup swerve
1 1/4 teaspoons salt
1 tablespoon instant yeast
How to prepare:
Start by preparing and preheating oven at 350 degrees F.
First, whisk all the dry bun ingredients in a mixing bowl.
Beat the remaining wet ingredients in another bowl until foamy.
Gradually add the dry flour mixture with constant mixing.
Mix and knead well to form a soft and smooth dough.
Cover the dough with plastic wrap and leave for 30 minutes.
Divide the prepared dough into medium-sized 8 buns.
Place the buns in a greased baking sheet and flatten them slightly.
Bake the buns for 18 minutes approximately until done.
Serve warm and fresh.

Nutritional Values:

Calories 201
Total Fat 12.2 g
Saturated Fat 2.4 g
Cholesterol 110 mg
Sodium 276 mg
Total Carbs 4.3 g
Fiber 0.9 g
Sugar 1.4 g
Protein 8.8 g

Steamed Bao Buns

Preparation time: 10 minutes
Cooking time: 8 minutes
Servings: 18
Ingredients:
3 cups almond flour
1½ tablespoon swerve, plus a pinch
1 teaspoon fast-action dried yeast
1.6 oz. almond milk
1 tablespoon sunflower oil
1 tablespoon rice vinegar
1 teaspoon baking powder
How to prepare:
Start by preparing and preheating oven at 400 degrees F.
First, whisk all the dry bun ingredients in a mixing bowl.
Beat the remaining wet ingredients in another bowl until foamy.
Gradually add the dry flour mixture with constant mixing.
Mix and knead well to form a soft and smooth dough.
Cover the dough with plastic wrap and leave for 15 minutes.
Divide the prepared dough into medium-sized 18 buns.
Place the buns in a greased baking sheet and flatten them slightly.
Prepare and preheat the steamer, then place the buns in the steamer basket.
Steam the buns for 8 minutes until al dente.
Serve warm and fresh.

Nutritional Values:
Calories 272
Total Fat 18 g
Saturated Fat 5 g
Cholesterol 6.1 mg
Sodium 3 mg
Total Carbs 4 g
Fiber 3 g
Sugar 4 g
Protein 0.4 g

Hamburger Buns

Preparation time: 10 minutes
Cooking time: 18 minutes
Servings: 8
Ingredients:
1 tablespoon active dry yeast
1/2 cup warm water
1/2 cup almond milk
1 large egg
2 tablespoons vegetable oil
2 tablespoons swerve
1 teaspoon salt
3 cups almond flour
1 tablespoon butter
How to prepare:
Start by preparing and preheating oven at 375 degrees F.
First, whisk all the dry bun ingredients in a mixing bowl.
Beat the remaining wet ingredients in another bowl until foamy.
Gradually add the dry flour mixture with constant mixing.
Mix and knead well to form a soft and smooth dough.
Cover the dough with a plastic wrap and leave for 1 hour.
Divide the prepared dough into medium-sized 8 buns.
Place the buns in a greased baking sheet and flatten them slightly.
Bake the buns for 18 minutes approximately until done.
Serve warm and fresh.

Nutritional Values:
Calories 272
Total Fat 18 g
Saturated Fat 5 g
Cholesterol 6.1 mg
Sodium 3 mg
Total Carbs 4 g
Fiber 3 g
Sugar 4 g
Protein 0.4 g

Hot Cross Buns

Preparation time: 10 minutes
Cooking time: 27 minutes
Servings: 14
Ingredients:
3/4 cup almond milk
2 1/4 teaspoons active dry yeast
1 teaspoon granulated swerve
1/2 cup brown swerve
5 tablespoons unsalted butter, softened
1/2 teaspoon vanilla extract
2 large eggs, at room temperature
1 teaspoon salt
1 and 1/4 teaspoons ground cinnamon
1/2 teaspoon ground nutmeg
1/2 teaspoon ground allspice
3 and 1/2 cups almond flour
1 cup raisins
Flour Cross
1/2 cup almond flour
8 tablespoons water
1 cup confectioners' swerve
3 tablespoons almond milk
How to prepare:
Start by preparing and preheating oven at 350 degrees F.
First, whisk all the dry bun ingredients in a mixing bowl.
Beat the remaining wet ingredients in another bowl until foamy.
Gradually add the dry flour mixture with constant mixing.
Mix and knead well to form a soft and smooth dough.
Cover the dough with plastic wrap and leave for 2 hours.
Divide the prepared dough into medium-sized 16 buns.
Place the buns in a greased baking sheet and flatten them slightly.
Bake the buns for 25 minutes approximately until done.
Meanwhile, prepare the icing by heating its ingredient in a saucepan for 2 minutes.
Drizzle this icing over the baked buns.
Serve warm and fresh.

Nutritional Values:
Calories 104
Total Fat 8.9 g
Saturated Fat 4.5 g
Cholesterol 57 mg
Sodium 340 mg
Total Carbs 4.7 g
Fiber 1.2 g
Sugar 1.3 g
Protein 3.3g

Pistachio Buns

Preparation time: 10 minutes
Cooking time: 15 minutes
Servings: 12
Ingredients:
Filling:
7 1/2 oz. homemade pistachio paste
2 ounces unsalted butter
Dough:
18 oz. almond flour
2 teaspoons instant yeast
2 teaspoons salt
10 oz. homemade pistachio paste
8 ounces plain, unsweetened Greek yogurt
4 oz. almond milk
2 ounces roasted pistachio oil
4 ounces blanched, peeled, and toasted pistachios
For the Frosting:
6 oz. heavy cream
2 1/2 ounces chilled homemade pistachio paste
How to prepare:
Start by preparing the filling in a mixer.

Add butter, pistachio paste to a food processor and blend well until smooth.

Transfer this filling to a piping bag and refrigerate until needed.

Prepare the dough by whisking all its dry ingredients in a bowl.

Separately beat the wet ingredients then gradually stir in the dry mixture.

Mix well and knead to form a smooth and elastic dough.

Cover this dough with a plastic wrap and let it sit for 2 hours.

Knead the dough again then spread it into a 13-inch square sheet.

Spread the pistachio filling over the dough sheet.

Start rolling the sheet into a log then slice this log into 12 thick rounds.

If desired, sprinkle additional pistachios over the filling.

Place the dough slices on a baking sheet and cover with an aluminum foil.

Place the rolls in the refrigerator for overnight.

Meanwhile, prepare the frosting by mixing pistachio paste with cream in a blender jug.

Uncover the refrigerated rolls and bake for 15 minutes the oven at 350 degrees F.

Serve with a dollop of prepared frosting on top.

Nutritional Values:
Calories 121
Total Fat 12.2 g
Saturated Fat 2.4 g
Cholesterol 110 mg
Sodium 276 mg
Total Carbs 3 g
Fiber 0.9 g
Sugar 1.4 g
Protein 1.8 g

Zesty Buns

Preparation time: 10 minutes
Cooking time: 20 minutes
Servings: 12
Ingredients:
Dough
1 ¼-ounce envelope active dry yeast
1 cup almond milk, warmed
1 teaspoon ¼ cup sugar-free maple syrup
4 large eggs, separated, plus 1 large egg yolk
3½ cups almond flour, divided
1 cup coconut flour
2 teaspoons salt
2 teaspoons finely grated orange zest
2 teaspoons vanilla extract
1 cup unsalted butter, diced
Filling and Assembly
¾ cup brown swerve
1 tablespoon ground cinnamon
¾ teaspoon ground cardamom
½ cup sugar-free maple syrup, divided
12 tablespoons (1½ sticks) unsalted butter, divided
Almond flour (for surface)
Nonstick vegetable oil spray
granulated swerve (for sprinkling)
How to prepare:
Take a large saucepan and add butter and almond milk.
Put this mixture over medium heat and cook for 30 seconds.
Remove it from the heat then stir in yeast, sweetener, and salt.
Mix well and leave it for 10 minutes approximately.
Continue adding remaining ingredients while mixing continuously.
Mix well to form a dough then cover it. Keep aside for 8 hours.
Separately mix all the ingredients for glaze in a bowl.
Now spread the prepared dough into a thin rectangle sheet and spread the filling over it.
Spread the prepared filling over the dough sheet then roll it.

Slice the dough into thick slices then place them in a greased baking sheet.
Bake for 20 minutes approximately at 350 degrees F.
Once buns turn golden brown, allow them to cool.
Serve.

Nutritional Values:
Calories 192
Total Fat 11.8 g
Saturated Fat 3.9 g
Cholesterol 135 mg
Sodium 187 mg
Total Carbs 4.1 g
Fiber 0.1g
Sugar 2.1 g
Protein 5.9 g

Brioche Buns

Preparation time: 10 minutes
Cooking time: 20 minutes
Servings: 8
Ingredients:
1 cup of warm water
3 tablespoons warm almond milk
2 teaspoons active dry yeast
2 1/2 tablespoons sugar
2 large eggs
3 cups bread flour
1/3 cup all-purpose flour
1 1/2 teaspoons salt
2 1/2 tablespoons unsalted butter, softened.
sesame seeds for topping
How to prepare:
Start by preparing and preheating oven at 400 degrees F.
First, whisk all the dry bun ingredients in a mixing bowl.
Beat 1 egg with remaining wet ingredients in another bowl until foamy.
Gradually add the dry flour mixture with constant mixing.
Mix and knead well for 8 minutes to form a soft and smooth dough.
Cover the dough with plastic wrap and leave for 2 hours.

Divide the prepared dough into medium-sized 8 buns.
Place the buns in a greased baking sheet and flatten them slightly.
Whisk one egg with a tablespoon of water and brush over the buns.
Drizzle the sesame seeds on top.
Bake the buns for 20 minutes approximately until done.
Serve warm and fresh.

Nutritional Values:
Calories 172
Total Fat 10.7 g
Saturated Fat 7.4 g
Cholesterol 62 mg
Sodium 121 mg
Total Carbs 4.9 g
Fiber 0.6 g
Sugar 17.3 g
Protein 4 g

Fluffy Psyllium Buns

Preparation time: 10 minutes
Cooking time: 25 minutes
Servings: 4
Ingredients:
3 egg whites
1 egg
1/4 cup hot water
1/4 cup almond flour
1/4 cup coconut flour
1 tablespoon psyllium husk powder
1 teaspoon baking powder
sesame seeds, for sprinkling optional
How to prepare:
Start by preparing and preheating oven at 356 degrees F.
First, whisk all the dry bun ingredients in a mixing bowl.
Beat the remaining wet ingredients in another bowl until foamy.
Gradually add the dry flour mixture with constant mixing.
Mix and knead well for 8 minutes to form a soft and smooth dough.
Cover the dough with plastic wrap and leave for 2 hours.
Divide the prepared dough into medium-sized 4 buns.
Place the buns in a greased baking sheet and flatten them slightly.
Drizzle seeds over these buns and carve a cross on top of the bun.
Bake the buns for 25 minutes approximately until done.
Serve warm and fresh.

Nutritional Values:
Calories 198
Total Fat 19.2 g
Saturated Fat 11.5 g
Cholesterol 123 mg
Sodium 142 mg
Total Carbs 4.5 g
Sugar 3.3 g
Fiber 0.3 g
Protein 3.4 g

Norwegian Buns

Preparation time: 10 minutes
Cooking time: 25 minutes
Servings: 20
Ingredients:
4 cups almond flour
¾ cup swerve
½ teaspoon salt
1/3 oz. sachets/envelopes easy-blend yeast
1/3 cup unsalted butter
1 ¾ cup almond milk
2 eggs
FOR THE FILLING
1 cup unsalted butter
1 cup swerve
1½ teaspoons cinnamon
1 egg (beaten), to glaze
How to prepare:
Start by preparing and preheating oven at 450 degrees F.
First, whisk all the dry bun ingredients in a mixing bowl.
Beat the remaining wet ingredients in another bowl until foamy.
Gradually add the dry flour mixture with constant mixing.
Mix and knead well for 8 minutes to form a soft and smooth dough.
Cover the dough with plastic wrap and leave for 2 hours.
Divide the prepared almond dough into three equal portions.
Spread each portion into a 9x13 inches sheet.
Whisk all the ingredients for filling in a bowl.
Top the rectangle dough sheets with this filling.
Roll the rectangle sheet into a log, and slice them into ¾ inch slices.
Place these buns in a greased baking sheet.
Brush them with whisked eggs on top and leave for 15 minutes.
Now bake the buns for 25 minutes until golden brown.
Serve warm and fresh.

Nutritional Values:

Calories 175
Total Fat 16 g
Saturated Fat 2.1 g
Cholesterol 124 mg
Sodium 8 mg
Total Carbs 2.8 g
Sugar 1.8 g
Fiber 0.4 g
Protein 9 g

Butterfly Buns

Preparation time: 10 minutes
Cooking time: 20 minutes
Servings: 8
Ingredients:
4oz swerve
4oz butter softened
2 large eggs
4oz almond flour
½ teaspoon baking powder
1tablespoon almond milk
2oz butter softened
3oz swerve
2tablespoon sugar-free strawberry jam
Swerve, for dusting
How to prepare:
Start by preparing and preheating oven at 400 degrees F.
First, whisk all the dry bun ingredients in a mixing bowl.
Beat the remaining wet ingredients in another bowl until foamy.
Gradually add the dry flour mixture with constant mixing.
Mix and knead well for 8 minutes to form a soft and smooth dough.
Cover the dough with plastic wrap and leave for 2 hours.
Divide the prepared dough into medium-sized 8 buns.
Place the buns in a greased baking sheet and flatten them slightly.
Bake the buns for 20 minutes approximately until done.
Take a bun and slice its top off.
Add sugar-free jam and sweetener to the center of the bun.
Cut the tops in half and arrange them over the buns like butterfly wings.
Serve warm and fresh.

Nutritional Values
Calories 167
Total Fat 5.1 g
Saturated Fat 1.1 g
Cholesterol 121 mg
Sodium 48 mg

Total Carbs 8.9 g
Sugar 3.8 g
Fiber 2.1 g
Protein 6.3 g

Sticky Cinnamon Buns

Preparation time: 10 minutes
Cooking time: 30 minutes
Servings: 08
Ingredients:
Dough
1 cup almond milk
1½ teaspoon dry yeast
¼ cup swerve
2oz butter, melted
3 cups almond flour
½ teaspoon salt
Cinnamon Filling
3¼oz butter softened
½ cup swerve
1 tablespoon ground cinnamon
Syrup Glaze
¼ cup swerve
3 tablespoon water
¾ cup swerve for icing
4-5 teaspoon water

How to prepare:
Take a large saucepan and add butter and almond milk.
Put this mixture over medium heat and cook for 30 seconds.
Remove it from the heat then stir in yeast, sweetener, and salt.
Mix well and leave it for 10 minutes approximately.
Continue adding remaining ingredients while mixing continuously.
Mix well to form a dough then cover it. Keep aside for 8 hours.
Separately mix all the ingredients for glaze in a bowl.
Now spread the prepared dough into a thin rectangle sheet and spread the filling over it.
Spread the prepared filling over the dough sheet then roll it.
Slice the dough into thick slices then place them in a greased baking sheet.
Bake for 25 minutes approximately at 350 degrees F.
Once buns turn golden brown, allow them to cool.
Meanwhile, whisk all the ingredients for the syrup in a saucepan.

Cook this syrup for 5 minutes until thick.
Drizzle this syrup over the buns.
Serve.

Nutritional Values:
Calories 236
Total Fat 13.5 g
Saturated Fat 4.2 g
Cholesterol 541 mg
Sodium 21 mg
Total Carbs 7.6 g
Sugar 1.4 g
Fiber 3.8 g
Protein 4.3 g

Steamed Pork Buns

Preparation time: 10 minutes
Cooking time: 30 minutes
Servings: 8
Ingredients:
Filling:
1/2 teaspoon five-spice powder
1-pound pork tenderloin, trimmed
Cooking spray
1 cup thinly sliced green onions
3 tablespoons hoisin sauce
2 tablespoons rice vinegar
1 tablespoon low-sodium soy sauce
1 1/2 teaspoons sugar-free maple syrup
1 teaspoon minced peeled fresh ginger
1 teaspoon minced garlic
1/4 teaspoon salt
Dough:
1 cup of warm water
3 tablespoons swerve
1 package dry yeast
3 1/4 cups almond flour
3 tablespoons canola oil
1/4 teaspoon salt
1 1/2 teaspoons baking powder
How to prepare:

First, prepare the filling of this bun by mixing pork with five-spice powder.

Place a suitable grill pan over medium heat and grease it with cooking spray.

Stir in pork and sauté for 10 minutes then remove it from the heat.

Add pork to a bowl along with onion and next seven ingredients in the list.

Mix well then cover this filling to refrigerate until needed.

Now prepare the dough by mixing 1 cup warm water, yeast and sweetener in a bowl then leave it for 5 minutes.

Whisk the remaining ingredients for the dough in another bowl.

Slowly in stir in yeast mixture and mix well until smooth.
Cover the dough with plastic wrap and leave it for 1 hour.
Knead the dough again and leave for another 5 minutes.
Divide this dough into 10 equal portions and spread all into a 5-inch circle.
Take the prepared filling and divide onto the circles.
Wrap the circles around their filling and seal it by pinching the edges together.
Place these buns in a bamboo steam basket with 1-inch distance in between.
Use a 2 tiered basket or cook them batches.
Fill a large pot with water up to its 1/3 full.
Place the steamer basket over it and let the water boil to steam.
Cover the buns and let them steam cook for 15 minutes.
Serve.

Nutritional Values:
Calories 121
Total Fat 12.9 g
Saturated Fat 5.1 g
Cholesterol 17 mg
Sodium 28 mg
Total Carbs 8.1 g
Sugar 1.8 g
Fiber 0.4 g
Protein 5.4 g

Chapter 8

Best Keto Recipes

Coffee Dessert

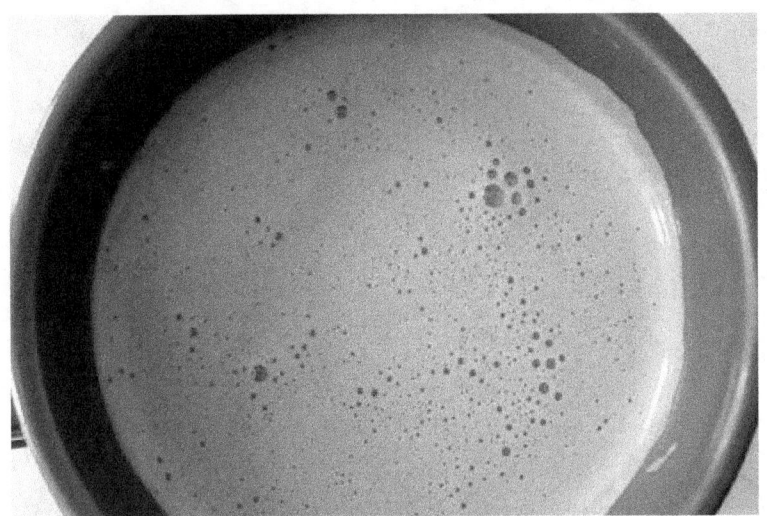

Preparation time: 5 minutes
Cooking Time: 5 minutes
Servings: 1

Ingredients:
2 tablespoons ground coffee
1 teaspoon ground cinnamon
2 cups of water
1/3 cup heavy whipping cream

Method:
Combine coffee with cinnamon in a bowl.

Stir in piping hot water and brew this mixture.
Beat cream in an electric mixer until foamy.
Pour the brewed coffee into the serving mug and top it with whipped cream.
Garnish with the cinnamon ground and serve.

Nutritional Values:
Calories 376
Total Fat 12.1 g
Saturated Fat 14.2 g
Cholesterol 195 mg
Sodium 73 mg
Total Carbs 4.6 g
Fiber 3.1 g
Sugar 2.1 g
Protein 5.7 g

Creamy Panna Cotta

Preparation time: 10 minutes
Cooking Time: 0 minutes
Servings: 4

Ingredients:
2 teaspoons unflavored powdered gelatin
Water (to dissolve gelatin)
2 cups heavy whipping cream
1 tablespoon vanilla extract
2 tablespoons pomegranates, the seeds
fresh mint (optional)

Method:
Mix gelatin with cold water in a bowl and mix well. Set it aside.

Mix cream with vanilla extract in a saucepan. Bring the mixture to a boil.

Cook on low heat until it thickens.

Turn off the heat and stir in gelatin.

Stir well until gelatin is completely mixed.

Divide the mixture in the serving glasses and cover with plastic wrap.

Refrigerate overnight then garnish with fresh mint and pomegranate seeds.

Serve.

Nutritional Values:
Calories 265
Total Fat 26.1 g
Saturated Fat 7.8 g
Cholesterol 143 mg
Sodium 65 mg
Total Carbs 5.9 g
Fiber 3.2 g
Sugar 1.3 g
Protein 6.1 g

Spiced Panna Cotta

Preparation time: 10 minutes
Cooking Time: 0 minutes
Servings: 6

Ingredients:
½ tablespoon unflavored powdered gelatin
Water (to dissolve gelatin)
2 cups heavy whipping cream
¼ teaspoon vanilla extract
1 pinch saffron
1 tablespoon chopped almonds
12 physalis or fresh raspberries

Method:
Mix gelatin with cold water in a bowl and mix well. Set it aside.
Mix cream with vanilla extract and saffron in a saucepan. Boil the mixture.
Reduce the heat to a simmer and let it simmer until it thickens.
Turn off the heat and stir in gelatin.
Stir well until gelatin is completely mixed.

Divide the mixture in the serving glasses and cover with plastic wrap. Refrigerate overnight then garnish with toasted almonds and berries. Serve.

Nutritional Values:
Calories 347
Total Fat 11.6 g
Saturated Fat 2.3 g
Cholesterol 421 mg
Sodium 54 mg
Total Carbs 6.3 g
Fiber 0.6 g
Sugar 1.1 g
Protein 2.4 g

Coconut Vanilla Custard
Preparation time: 10 minutes
Cooking time: 50 minutes
Servings: 03

Ingredients:
3 eggs
1/2 teaspoon liquid stevia
dash salt
2 1/4 cups coconut milk
1/2 teaspoon vanilla extract
2 tablespoons unsweetened shredded coconut
dash ground nutmeg optional
How to prepare:
Mix eggs, sweetener, and salt until the eggs until well blended.
Add coconut milk to a pot and bring it just to a simmer.
Pour this coconut milk gradually into the eggs mixture.
Stir in vanilla extract and coconut.
Divide the batter into 5 custard cups and top it with nutmeg.
Keep these cups in a 13x9 baking dish and fill it with ½ cup water.
Bake for 50 mins at 350 degrees F in a preheated oven.
Allow the custard to cool then serve.

Nutritional Values:
Calories 345
Total Fat 27.2 g
Saturated Fat 15.2 g
Cholesterol 53 mg
Sodium 65 mg
Total Carbs 3.9 g
Fiber 1.2 g
Sugar 0.9 g
Protein 6.4 g

Eggnog Dessert

Preparation time: 10 minutes
Cooking Time: 0 minutes
Servings: 4

Ingredients:
2 egg yolks
½ teaspoon erythritol
¼ tablespoon vanilla extract
1 lemon, juice and zest
4 tablespoons brandy
1 cup heavy whipping cream
1 pinch ground nutmeg
Method:
Beat egg yolks with sweetener and vanilla powder until fluffy.
Stir in lemon zest, brandy, and lemon juice. Mix well.
Beat cream in another bowl. Add cream to the egg batter
Pour this batter into serving glasses and refrigerate for 15 minutes.
Garnish with nutmeg and serve.

Nutritional Values:
Calories 401
Total Fat 13.3 g
Saturated Fat 10.1 g
Cholesterol 43 mg
Sodium 54 mg
Total Carbs 15.3 g
Fiber 1.8 g
Sugar 1.4 g
Protein 4.7 g

Strawberry Coconut cream

Preparation time: 10 minutes
Cooking Time: 0 minutes
Servings: 1

Ingredients:
½ cup coconut cream
2 oz. fresh strawberries
1 pinch vanilla extract
Method:
Add all ingredients to a blender while keeping a few slices of strawberries.
Blend until smooth.
Transfer the dessert to the serving glass and top it with strawberries.
Refrigerate for 20 to 30 minutes.
Serve and enjoy.

Nutritional Values:
Calories 253
Total Fat 23.8 g
Saturated Fat 11.2 g
Cholesterol 212 mg
Sodium 47 mg
Total Carbs 4.7 g
Fiber 0.4 g
Sugar 6.3 g
Protein 7.1 g

Chocolate Vanilla mousse

Preparation time: 10 minutes
Cooking Time: 0 minutes
Servings: 6

Ingredients:
27 oz. coconut milk
3 tablespoons cocoa powder
1 teaspoon vanilla extract
1 teaspoon erythritol (optional)

Method:
Keep the coconut milk in the refrigerator for 4 hours until its cream separates from water.

Carefully scoop out the milk cream in a bowl and keep the water aside.

Beat coconut cream with sweetener and vanilla using a hand mixer, until it thickens.

Stir in cocoa powder and blend again.

Serve fresh in the dessert bowls.

Nutritional Values:
Calories 382
Total Fat 15.2 g
Saturated Fat 6.2 g
Cholesterol 133 mg
Sodium 76 mg
Total Carbs 6.2 g
Fiber 2.3 g
Sugar 1.7 g
Protein 4.1 g

Berry Mousse

Preparation time: 10 minutes
Cooking Time: 20 minutes
Servings: 16

Ingredients:
Dark chocolate cake
9 oz. dark chocolate with a minimum of 70% cocoa solids
5 oz. butter
5 eggs
1 pinch salt
1 teaspoon vanilla extract
For serving
2 cups fresh raspberries or fresh blueberries
1 teaspoon vanilla extract
6 tablespoons lime juice
4 oz. pecans, chopped
½ cup toasted unsweetened coconut chips
2 cups heavy whipping cream or crème Fraiche

Method:
Adjust your oven to 320 degrees F.

Butter a 9-inch springform pan and line it's base with parchment paper.

Add chocolate pieces and diced butter to a bowl. Microwave for few seconds and stir well to mix.

Beat egg whites with salt in a bowl using a hand blender until it forms peaks.

Whisk egg yolks with vanilla until smooth.

Add melted chocolate to the egg yolks and mix well.

Fold in fluffy egg whites and mix well.

Pour the batter into the pan then bake for 20 minutes.

For serving

Mix berries with lime juice and vanilla in a bowl. Set it aside.

Beat cream in a mixing bowl until it forms soft peaks.

Divide the cake into small pieces using your hand.

Add cake pieces to the serving plate and add berries, nuts, and coconut flakes.

Top them with whipped cream.

Serve.

Nutritional Values:
Calories 344

Total Fat 22.7 g
Saturated Fat 11.4 g
Cholesterol 144 mg
Sodium 54 mg
Total Carbs 3.1 g
Fiber 1.2 g
Sugar 0.6 g
Protein 5.2 g

Chapter 9

Ketogenic Dessert Bread

Cherry Chocolate Bread

Preparation time: 10 minutes
Cooking time: 50 minutes
Servings: 8
Ingredients:
1¼ cup almond flour
1/3 cup unsweetened cocoa
1/2 teaspoon sea salt
1 teaspoon baking powder
3/4 cup swerve
1/4 cup butter, softened
2 large eggs
3/4 cup almond milk
1/4 cup plain Greek yogurt
1/4 cup cherry
glaze
1 tablespoon pureed maraschino cherries
1 cup powdered Swerve
1-2 tablespoons maraschino cherry juice
1/4-1/2 cup cherry
How to prepare:
Start by preparing and preheating the oven at 350 degrees F.
Whisk cocoa with flour, baking powder and salt in a bowl.
Beat swerve with butter, milk, yogurt, and eggs in a separate mixing bowl.
Slowly add the dry ingredients while mixing well.
Spread this batter in a loaf pan greased with nonstick.
Top the batter with ¼ cup cherry and press it gently.

Bake for 50 minutes approximately.

Glaze
Meanwhile, prepare the glaze by blending all of its ingredients.
Top the baked bread with prepared glaze.
Slice and serve.

Nutritional Values:
Calories 179
Total Fat 15.7 g
Saturated Fat 8 g
Cholesterol 323mg
Sodium 43 mg
Total Carbs 4.8 g
Sugar 3.6 g
Fiber 0.8 g
Protein 5.6 g

Bread with Raspberry Butter

Preparation time: 10 minutes
Cooking time: 45 minutes
Servings: 12
Ingredients:
3 tablespoons coconut oil, divided
1/2 cup finely chopped pecans
1 1/2 teaspoons cinnamon, divided
1/3 cup + 1 tablespoon coconut sugar, divided
1 cup coconut flour
1/2 cup almond flour
1 teaspoon baking powder
1/2 teaspoon baking soda
1/2 teaspoon salt
2 avocados, mashed
2 eggs
1 teaspoon vanilla extract
2 tablespoons plain Greek yogurt
For the Butter
4 tablespoons unsalted butter, room temperature
1/4 cup raspberries

How to prepare:
Start by preparing and preheating the oven at 350 degrees F.
Melt coconut oil in a small skillet placed over medium heat.
Stir in 1 tablespoon coconut sugar, 1 teaspoon cinnamon, and pecans, sauté for 5 minutes.
Now whisk baking powder with flours, salt, baking soda, coconut sugar and cinnamon in a large bowl.
Beat the wet ingredients in a mixer then slowly add the dry mixture.
Fold in a toasted pecans mixture then spread the batter in a loaf pan.
Bake this pecan batter for 45 minutes approximately.
For the Butter
Meanwhile, mash raspberries with butter in a small bowl.
Spread this mixture over the baked bread.
Slice and serve.

Nutritional Values:
Calories 139
Total Fat 4.6 g
Saturated Fat 0.5 g
Cholesterol 1.2 mg
Sodium 83 mg
Total Carbs 7.5 g
Sugar 6.3 g
Fiber 0.6 g
Protein 3.8 g

Bread with Lime Glaze

Preparation time: 10 minutes
Cooking time: 50 minutes
Servings: 12
Ingredients:
coconut bread
1½ cups almond flour
1/2 teaspoon sea salt
1 teaspoon baking powder
3/4 cup swerve
1/4 cup butter, softened
2 large eggs
3/4 cup silk unsweetened coconut milk
1/2 teaspoon vanilla extract
1/3 cup sweetened flaked coconut
glaze/topping
1 cup powdered Swerve
1½ tablespoons fresh lime juice
1/3 cup sweetened flaked coconut
zest of 1 lime
How to prepare:
Start by preparing and preheating the oven at 350 degrees F.

Whisk all the dry ingredients in a bowl.
Beat the wet ingredients separately in a mixer.
Stir in dry mixture and mix well then fold in coconut flakes.
Spread this batter in a greased loaf pan.
Bake the dessert bread for 50 minutes approximately.
Glaze/Topping
Meanwhile, prepare the glaze by whisking all its ingredients.
Spread this glaze over the baked bread.
Serve.

Nutritional Values:
Calories 261
Total Fat 7.1 g
Saturated Fat 13.4 g
Cholesterol 0.3 mg
Sodium 10 mg
Total Carbs 6.1 g
Sugar 2.1 g
Fiber 3.9 g
Protein 1.8 g

Cream Cheese Filled Bread

Preparation time: 10 minutes
Cooking time: 20 minutes
Servings: 4
Ingredients:
1 (8-ounce) container sour cream
1/2 cup swerve
1/2 cup butter
1 teaspoon salt
4 1/2 teaspoons dry yeast
1/2 cup warm water
2 eggs, beaten
4 cups almond flour
Filling
2 (8-ounce) packages cream cheese, softened
3/4 cup swerve
1 egg, beaten
2 teaspoons vanilla extract
Glaze
2 cups powdered swerve
1/4 cup almond milk
2 teaspoons vanilla extract
How to prepare:
First, start by preparing the filling in a saucepan.

Add butter and melt it with sweetener, sour cream, and salt over medium heat.

Mix well then allow it to cool at room temperature.

Whisk yeast with warm water in a mixing bowl and let it rest for 5 minutes.

Stir in eggs and sour cream mixture with constant mixing.

Slowly add flour and mix until it forms a smooth dough then cover.

Refrigerate the dough for 8 hours until set.

Divide this dough into 4 equal parts.

Spread each part into 12x8 inch rectangles.

Top each rectangle with the filling while leaving ½ inch border.

Fold the rectangles and pinch the sides to seal the filling.

Place the rectangles on a baking sheet and bake for 20 minutes at 375 degrees F.

Serve with prepared glaze on top.

Nutritional Values:
Calories 151
Total Fat 14.7 g
Saturated Fat 1.5 g
Cholesterol 13 mg
Sodium 53 mg
Total Carbs 1.5 g
Sugar 0.3 g
Fiber 0.1 g
Protein 0.8 g

Nutmeg Eggnog Bread

Preparation time: 10 minutes
Cooking time: 60 minutes
Servings: 12
Ingredients:
Bread
1/2 cup butter, softened
1/2 cup swerve
1/2 cup brown swerve
1 teaspoon rum extract
1 egg
2 cups flour
1 1/2 teaspoon baking powder
1/2 teaspoon baking soda
1 teaspoon salt
1 teaspoon nutmeg
1 cup eggnog
The Glaze
1 cup powdered Swerve
2 tablespoons eggnog
pinch of nutmeg
How to prepare:
Start by preparing and preheating the oven at 350 degrees F.
Whisk all the dry ingredients in a bowl.
Beat the wet ingredients separately in a mixer.
Stir in dry mixture and mix well.
Spread this batter in a greased loaf pan.
Bake the dessert bread for 60 minutes approximately.
Slice and serve.

Nutritional Values:
Calories 195
Total Fat 14.3 g
Saturated Fat 10.5 g
Cholesterol 175 mg
Sodium 125 mg
Total Carbs 4.5 g
Sugar 0.5 g
Fiber 0.3 g
Protein 3.2 g

Cranberry Bliss Bread

Preparation time: 10 minutes
Cooking time: 56 minutes
Servings: 12
Ingredients:
1 cup almond flour
1/2 cup coconut flour
1/4 teaspoon baking soda
1/4 teaspoon baking powder
1/2 teaspoon salt
1/2 cup unsalted butter
1 cup swerve
2 large eggs
1 teaspoon vanilla extract
1/2 cup almond milk
1/2 cup dried cranberries
1/2 cup white sugar-free chocolate chips
frosting
2 cups swerve, sifted
1 teaspoon vanilla extract
cream to thin
drizzle
1/2 cup sugar-free white chocolate chips
1 teaspoon coconut or vegetable oil
How to prepare:
Start by preparing and preheating the oven at 350 degrees F.

Whisk all the dry bread ingredients together in a separate bowl.
Now beat butter with sweetener in a bowl until foamy.
Slowly whisk in eggs and vanilla, then beat until smooth.
Stir in the dry flour mixture along with almond milk.
Mix well until smooth then fold in cranberries and chocolate chips.
Spread this batter into a 9x5 inch loaf pan, layered with parchment sheet.
Bake the cranberry batter for 55 minutes approximately.
Meanwhile prepare the frosting by whisking cream with sweetener, and vanilla.
Spread this frosting over the baked cake and garnish with cranberries.
Melt chocolate in a bowl by heating in the microwave for 30 seconds.
Drizzle this chocolate over the cake frosting in a crisscross pattern.
Slice and serve.

Nutritional Values:
Calories 193
Total Fat 10 g
Saturated Fat 13.2 g
Cholesterol 120 mg
Sodium 8 mg
Total Carbs 2.5 g
Sugar 1 g
Fiber 0.7 g
Protein 2.2 g

Lemon Drop Bread

Preparation time: 10 minutes
Cooking time: 63 minutes
Servings: 12
Ingredients:
Bread
1 2/3 cups flour
1 teaspoon baking powder
1/2 teaspoon salt
4 tablespoon butter
1/2 cup yogurt
2 eggs
1 teaspoon grated lemon peel
1/4 cup limoncello
1/2 cup coconut milk
Glaze
Juice of 1 lemon
1/2 cup swerve
1 tablespoon limoncello
Candied lemon slices
1 lemon, thinly sliced
1 cup swerve
1 tablespoon limoncello
How to prepare:
Start by preparing and preheating the oven at 350 degrees F.

Meanwhile, grease a loaf pan with cooking oil and keep it aside.

Whisk all the dry ingredients in a separate bowl.

Beat butter with eggs, limoncello, coconut milk and yogurt in a mixing bowl.

Slow stir in flour mixture and the lemon peel then mix well until smooth.

Evenly spread this lemon batter in the prepared pan.

Bake for 60 minutes approximately until golden brown.

Meanwhile, prepare the lemon glaze by whisking all its ingredients in a saucepan.

Boil for 3 minutes on medium heat until it bubbles.

Whisk lemon slices with swerve and limoncello in a bowl.

Spread these slices in a baking tray and bake them for 10 minutes.

Place these lemon slices over the baked bread then drizzle the glaze on top.

Allow it to set then slice to serve.

Nutritional Values:
Calories 136
Total Fat 10.7 g
Saturated Fat 0.5 g
Cholesterol 4 mg
Sodium 45 mg
Total Carbs 1.2 g
Sugar 1.4 g
Fiber 0.2 g
Protein 0.9

Chocolate Peppermint Bread

Preparation time: 10 minutes
Cooking time: 61 minutes
Servings: 12
Ingredients:
½ cup butter
1½ cups swerve
¾ teaspoon salt
1 teaspoon vanilla extract
1 teaspoon peppermint extract
½ teaspoon baking powder
⅔ cup of cocoa powder
3 eggs
1¼ cup flour
¾ cup almond milk
⅓ cup Andes peppermint crunch chips, plus more for garnish
How to prepare:
Start by preparing and preheating the oven at 350 degrees F.
Grease a 9x5 inch loaf pan with cooking spray.
Whisk butter with salt, sweetener, baking powder, cocoa powder and extracts in a mixing bowl.
Stir in eggs and continue whisking until well incorporated.
Gradually add the flour with constant mixing.
Spread this batter in the prepared pan evenly then bake for 60 minutes approximately.
Melt the peppermint chips in a bowl by heating in the microwave for 30 seconds.
Spread this melt over the baked dessert.
Alternatively spread the peppermint chips over the bread.
Slice and serve.
Nutritional Values:
Calories 200
Total Fat 11.1 g
Saturated Fat 9.5 g
Cholesterol 124.2 mg
Sodium 46 mg
Total Carbs 1.1 g

Sugar 1.3 g
Fiber 0.4 g
Protein 0.4 g

Romanian Sweet Bread

Preparation time: 10 minutes
Cooking time: 0 minutes
Servings: 12
Ingredients:
dough:
4 cups almond flour
4 egg yolks
1 ¼ cups almond milk
1 ½ tablespoon vegetable oil
1 oz. fresh yeast
3.5 oz. butter
½ cup granulated Swerve
1 tablespoon rum
zest of ½ organic lemon
½ teaspoon salt
1 tablespoon vanilla swerve
filling:
2 egg whites
½ cup granulated Swerve
1 tablespoon rum
⅔ cup ground walnuts
How to prepare:
Whisk flour in a large bowl and stir in hot milk into the flour.
Mix well until smooth then allow it to cool.
Now mix yeast with sweetener in a small bowl.
Add this yeast mixture into the flour mixture.
After mixing this dough, cover it with a kitchen towel.
Keep it aside for 20 minutes at a warm place.
During this time mix melted butter with salt and egg yolks in a mixing bowl.
Stir in remaining bread ingredients and beat well until incorporated.

Add this egg mixture to the dry flour mixture and knead well for 15 minutes.

Leave the dough for 20 minutes then knead again.

Meanwhile, prepare and preheat the oven at 375 degrees F.

Grease two loaf pans with butter and keep them aside.

Prepare the filling by whisking 2 egg whites with sweetener and rum in a bowl.

Fold in walnuts and mix well.

Divide and spread the dough in two greased loaf pans.

Spread the prepared frosting on top.

Bake for 60 minutes approximately.

Slice and serve.

Nutritional Values:
Calories 113
Total Fat 9 g
Saturated Fat 0.2 g
Cholesterol 1.7 mg
Sodium 134 mg
Total Carbs 6.5 g
Sugar 1.8 g
Fiber 0.7 g
Protein 7.5 g

Snickerdoodle Bread

Preparation time: 10 minutes
Cooking time: 40 minutes
Servings: 12
Ingredients:
3 cups almond flour
2 teaspoons baking powder
1/2 teaspoon salt
2 teaspoons cinnamon
1 cup butter, softened
2 cup swerve
4 eggs
2 teaspoons vanilla
1 cup sour cream
1 1/2 cup cinnamon chips
2 tablespoons almond flour
2 tablespoons swerve
2 teaspoons cinnamon
How to prepare:
Start by preparing and preheating the oven at 350 degrees F.
Grease 5 mini loaf pans with cooking oil

Add 3 cups flour to a medium bowl then stir in salt, baking powder, and cinnamon.

Mix well then keep this dry mixture aside.

Beat butter with sweetener in a mixing bowl until fluffy.

Stir in eggs, vanilla and sour cream then mix until smooth.

Slowly add the dry flour mixture and mix until well incorporated.

Toss the cinnamon chips with 2 tablespoon flour in a bowl.

Evenly spread the bread batter in the greased pan and then top it with sweetener and cinnamon.

Bake for 40 minutes approximately then allow to cool.

Slice and serve.

Nutritional Values:
Calories 213
Total Fat 19 g
Saturated Fat 15.2 g
Cholesterol 13 mg
Sodium 52 mg
Total Carbs 5.5 g
Sugar 1.3 g
Fiber 0.5 g
Protein 6.1 g

Swedish Coffee Bread

Preparation time: 10 minutes
Cooking time: 30 minutes
Servings: 12
Ingredients:
Bread:
1 cup almond milk
1/2 cup swerve
1/2 cup butter
2-pkg active yeast mixed with 1/4 cup warm water
4 cups almond flour
1 large egg
1/2 teaspoon salt
1 teaspoon ground cardamom
Filling:
2 tablespoons melted butter
1/4 cup brown swerve, packed
1 tablespoon swerve
2 teaspoons cinnamon
1/2 cup slivered almonds
1/4 cup almond paste
Egg glaze:
2 egg yolks
2 tablespoon cream
How to prepare:
Start by pouring milk into a small pan and put it over medium heat.
Once the milk is warm, remove it from the heat then add sweetener and butter.
Pour this milk in a mixing bowl then add yeast and egg
Stir in cardamom and salt, then gradually add flour while whisking continuously.
Knead this cardamom dough on a floured surface for 10 minutes.
Add the dough in an oiled bowl then cover it with plastic wrap.
Keep this dough aside at a warm place for 1 hour.
Divide this dough in half and divide each half into three parts.
Roll each part into ropes then bread the three ropes together.
Place the breaded dough in a baking sheet.

Beat egg yolks with cream in a bowl then brush over the dough.
Bake the breaded bread for 30 minutes approximately.
Slice and serve.

Nutritional Values:
Calories 197
Total Fat 19.2 g
Saturated Fat 10.1 g
Cholesterol 11 mg
Sodium 78 mg
Total Carbs 7.3 g
Sugar 1.2 g
Fiber 0.8 g
Protein 4.2 g

Lemon Zucchini Bread

Preparation time: 10 minutes
Cooking time: 0 minutes
Servings: 01s
Ingredients:
Bread
2 cups almond flour
1/2 teaspoon salt
2 teaspoon baking powder
2 eggs
1/2 cup canola oil
1 1/3 cup swerve
2 tablespoon lemon juice
1/2 cup almond milk
1 lemon zest
1 cup zucchini grated
Glaze
1 cup powdered Swerve
2 tablespoon lemon juice
1 tablespoon almond milk
How to prepare:
Start by whisking the salt, with flour and baking powder in a medium bowl.

Beat eggs with oil, sweetener, lemon juice, lemon zest and almond milk in a large bowl.

Once well-mixed stir in zucchini and all other dry ingredients.

Whisk well until smooth then spread the batter in a 9x5 loaf pan.

Bake the bread for 45 minutes approximately at 350 degrees F.

Meanwhile, prepare the glaze by whisking all its ingredients.

Allow the baked bread to cool down completely.

Spread the prepared glaze on top.

Slice and serve.

Nutritional Values:
Calories 254
Total Fat 9 g
Saturated Fat 10.1 g
Cholesterol 13 mg

Sodium 179 mg
Total Carbs 7.5 g
Sugar 1.2 g
Fiber 0.8 g
Protein 7.5 g

Cream Filled Pumpkin Bread

Preparation time: 10 minutes
Cooking time: 55 minutes
Servings: 12
Ingredients:
Bread:
2 eggs
3/4 cup vegetable oil
1 cup swerve
1/4 cup brown swerve
1 teaspoon vanilla
15 oz. pumpkin puree
1 3/4 cups almond flour
2 teaspoons pumpkin pie spice
1 teaspoon baking soda
1/2 teaspoon ground cinnamon
1/2 teaspoon ground nutmeg
1/2 teaspoon salt
FILLING:
8 oz. cream cheese
3/4 cup powder swerve
How to prepare:
Start by preparing and preheating the oven at 350 degrees F.

Layer a 9x5 inch baking pan with cooking spray and keep it aside.

Now start beating eggs with sweetener, oil, and vanilla in a mixing bowl.

Gradually fold in other ingredients for bread while mixing continuously.

Beat cream cheese with sweetener then pour into a Ziploc bag with a cut tip.

Spread half of the batter in the prepared pan.

Top this batter with cream cheese filling.
Now spread the remaining half of the batter on top to cover the filling.
Bake this sandwich bread for 55 minutes approximately.
Allow the bread to cool down a little.
Slice and serve as desired.
-Nutritional Values:
Calories 290
Total Fat 21.5 g
Saturated Fat 15.2 g
Cholesterol 12.1 mg
Sodium 9 mg
Total Carbs 6.5 g
Sugar 1.2 g
Fiber 0.4 g
Protein 6.2 g

Pumpkin Pie Spice Loaf

Preparation time: 10 minutes
Cooking time: 60 minutes
Servings: 8
Ingredients:
½ cup brown swerve
½ cup swerve
1 cup canned pumpkin
⅓ cup canola oil
1 teaspoon vanilla
2 eggs
1½ cups almond flour
2 teaspoon baking powder
¼ teaspoon salt
1½ teaspoon pumpkin pie spice
½ cup chopped walnuts, optional
How to prepare:
Start by preparing and preheating the oven at 350 degrees F.
Layer an 8x4 inches pan with cooking oil.
Mix all the dry ingredients together in a separate bowl.
Beat the wet ingredients together in another bowl until smooth.
Spread this spice batter in the pans.
Bake the batter for 60 minutes approximately.
Slice and serve.

Nutritional Values:
Calories 214
Total Fat 19 g
Saturated Fat 5.8 g
Cholesterol 15 mg
Sodium 123 mg
Total Carbs 6.5 g
Sugar 1.9 g
Fiber 2.1 g
Protein 6.5 g

Poppy Seed Pound Cake

Preparation time: 10 minutes
Cooking time: 70 minutes
Servings: 12
Ingredients:
3/4 cup butter, softened
1 cup erythritol
4 large egg
3/4 cup sour cream
2 tablespoon lemon extract
2 teaspoon vanilla extract
3 cup blanched almond flour
2 teaspoons gluten-free baking powder
3 tablespoon poppy seeds
1/2 teaspoon Sea salt
Lemon Glaze
3/4 cup powdered erythritol
1/4 cup lemon juice
1/4 teaspoon vanilla extract
How to prepare:
Start by preparing and preheating the oven at 350 degrees F.
Grease a medium-sized Bundt pan and keep them aside.
Beat butter with sweetener in a mixer until fluffy.
Whisk in lemon extract, vanilla extract, sour cream, and eggs.
Continue beating until creamy in texture.
Separately mix the dry ingredients in a separate bowl.
Add this mixture to the wet ingredients and mix well until smooth.
Spread this batter in the Bundt pan and bake for 40 minutes in the oven.
Cover the cake with aluminum foil and bake for another 30 minutes.
Allow it to cool for 15 minutes.
Prepare the glaze by whisking all of its ingredients in a bowl.
Drizzle this glaze over the baked cake.
Slice and serve.

Nutritional Values:
Calories 331

Total Fat 38.5 g
Saturated Fat 19.2 g
Cholesterol 141 mg
Sodium 283 mg
Total Carbs 9.2 g
Sugar 3 g
Fiber 1 g
Protein 2.1 g

Tiramisu Poke Cake

Preparation time: 10 minutes
Cooking time: 3 hrs. 5 minutes
Servings: 12
Ingredients:
6 large eggs
1/2 cup melted butter
1/2 cup almond milk, lukewarm
2 cups almond flour
1/3 cup coconut flour
1/4 cup whey protein powder
1/3 cup granulated Erythritol
1/2 teaspoon baking soda
1 teaspoon cream of tartar
1/4 teaspoon sea salt
Coffee-rum custard filling:
4 egg yolks
3 tablespoon granulated erythritol
3/4 cup unsweetened almond milk
2 tablespoons heavy whipping cream
1/2 cup strong brewed coffee
1 teaspoon grass-fed gelatin powder
2 tablespoon water
1/4 cup dark rum
liquid stevia, to taste
Mascarpone topping:
2 large eggs, separated
1 tablespoon water

1/4 cup powdered erythritol
1/2 cup mascarpone
1 teaspoon sugar-free vanilla extract
1 tablespoon cacao powder

How to prepare:
First-line a slow cooker with parchment sheet and set on low heat.
Whisk all the wet ingredients in a bowl until smooth.
Mix all the dry ingredients separately.
Add this dry mixture to the wet mixture and mix well until smooth.
Spread this batter in the prepared slow cooker and cover it lid.
Cook the batter for 3 hours on slow cooking.
During this time, prepare the filling by beating its ingredients in a saucepan until fluffy.
Heat this coffee mixture to a simmer until it thickens.
Remove the glaze from the heat then pour this mixture into a glass bowl.
Refrigerate this mixture for 2 hours.
Now beat the ingredients for mascarpone topping in a bowl.
Heat the custard mixture in a saucepan and stir in mascarpone mixture.
Whisk well then allow it to cool.
Spread this mixture over the baked cake evenly.
Drizzle cocoa powder on top then slice.
Serve fresh.

Nutritional Values:
Calories 267
Total Fat 44.5 g
Saturated Fat 17.4 g
Cholesterol 153 mg
Sodium 217 mg
Total Carbs 8.4 g
Sugar 2.3 g
Fiber 1.3 g
Protein 3.1 g

Carrot Cake

Preparation time: 10 minutes
Cooking time: 40 minutes
Servings: 12
Ingredients:
2 3/4 cups almond flour
1 1/4 cups powdered erythritol
2 teaspoons gluten-free baking powder
2 teaspoon cinnamon
1/2 teaspoon sea salt
6 large eggs
1/2 cup melted butter
1/4 cup unsweetened almond milk
2 cups grated carrots
2 teaspoons sugar-free vanilla extract
1/2 cup pecan pieces
Frosting:
1 cup full-fat cream cheese
1 cup powdered erythritol
1/3 cup heavy whipping cream
1/2 cup pecan pieces, divided
How to prepare:
Start the preparing and preheating the oven at 350 degrees F.
Whisk the dry ingredients for the cake in a bowl.
Beat the wet ingredients separately in another bowl.
Stir in the dry mixture then mix well until smooth.
Fold in carrots and mix gently until well incorporated.
Spread this batter in a 9-inch pan layered with parchment sheet.
Bake this batter for 40 minutes approximately until all done.
Meanwhile, prepare the frosting by beating all of its ingredients.
Spread this topping over the baked cake.
Slice and serve.
Nutritional Values:
Calories 259
Total Fat 34 g
Saturated Fat 10.3 g
Cholesterol 112 mg

Sodium 92 mg
Total Carbs 8.5 g
Sugar 2 g
Fiber 1.3 g
Protein 7.5 g

Lemon Ricotta Cheesecake

Preparation time: 10 minutes
Cooking time: 15 minutes
Servings: 8
Ingredients:
Crust
2 cups almond flour
6 tablespoons unsalted butter
1/4 teaspoon sea salt
2 tablespoons low carb swerve substitute
Filling
16 oz. cream cheese softened
15 oz. ricotta cheese
1 cup low carb swerve substitute
1 tablespoon vanilla extract
2 teaspoons fresh lemon zest
1/2 teaspoon lemon extract
1 1/2 cups heavy cream
How to prepare:
Start by preparing and preheating the oven at 350 degrees F.

Add butter to a bowl and melt by heating in the microwave for 30 seconds.'

Stir in crust ingredients and mix well until fully incorporated.

Grease a 9-inch pie pan with cooking spray and spread the crust in the pie pan.

Bake this crust for 15 minutes approximately.

Filling
Meanwhile, beat the ingredients for filling in a mixer until creamy.
Add this filling to the baked crust and beat until creamy.
Spread this filling in the baked crust and refrigerate for 4 hours.
Slice and serve.

Nutritional Values:
Calories 255
Total Fat 23.4 g
Saturated Fat 11.7 g
Cholesterol 135 mg

Sodium 112 mg
Total Carbs 2.5 g
Sugar 12.5 g
Fiber 1 g
Protein 7.9 g

Decadent Cheesecake

Preparation time: 10 minutes
Cooking time: 1hr. 18 minutes
Servings: 12
Ingredients:
Crust:
4 tablespoon butter
1 1/2 cups almond flour
1/4 cup monk fruit sweetener
Filling:
3 8 oz. packages (24 oz.) cream cheese, softened
1 cup monk fruit sweetener
3 large eggs
1/4 cup heavy whipping cream
3/4 teaspoon pure vanilla extract
1/3 cup frozen raspberries
2 tablespoons heavy whipping cream
How to prepare:
Start by preparing and preheating the oven at 350 degrees F.
Add butter to a bowl and melt by heating in the microwave.
Whisk all the ingredients for the crust in a mixing bowl.
Spread this crust mixture in a 9-inch springform pan.
Bake this crust for 8 minutes until golden.
Meanwhile, beat the ingredients for filling together in a mixing bowl.
Add this filling to the baked crust and spread it evenly.
Switch the oven at 325 degrees F.
Bake the cake for 1 hour and 10 minutes until all done.
Refrigerate this cake for 4 hours.
Meanwhile, prepare the raspberry cream sauce by heating raspberries in the microwave.
Beat raspberries with cream in a bowl.

Spread this sauce over the cake.
Slice and serve.

Nutritional Values:
Calories 251
Total Fat 24.5 g
Saturated Fat 14.7 g
Cholesterol 165 mg
Sodium 142 mg
Total Carbs 4.3 g
Sugar 0.5 g
Fiber 1 g
Protein 5.9 g

Caramel Cake

Preparation time: 10 minutes
Cooking time: 30 minutes
Servings: 8
Ingredients:
2 1/2 cups almond flour
1/4 cup coconut flour
1/4 cup unflavored whey protein powder
1 tablespoon baking powder
1/2 teaspoon salt
1/2 cup butter softened
2/3 cup Swerve Sweetener
4 large eggs room temperature
1 teaspoon vanilla extract
3/4 cup almond milk
2 batches sugar-free caramel sauce
How to prepare:
Start by preparing and preheating the oven at 325 degrees F.
Grease two 8 inches round baking pans.
Layer the pans with parchment sheet.
Mix almond flour with baking powder, salt, why protein and coconut flour in a medium bowl.
Now beat the butter with sweetener in another bowl until fluffy.

Stir in eggs and whisk well then add vanilla extract.

Slowly add the dry mixture along with almond milk while beating continuously.

Divide this prepared batter in the cake pans and bake for 25 minutes approximately.

Caramel Glaze:

Meanwhile, prepare the caramel sauce by whisking all its ingredients in a saucepan.

Cook until it thickens then allow it to cool.

Spread ½ of this sauce over one cake then place other cake on top.

Drizzle the remaining sauce on top and spread it evenly.

Slice and serve.

Nutritional Values:
Calories 195
Total Fat 13 g
Saturated Fat 5 g
Cholesterol 132 mg
Sodium 297 mg
Total Carbs 11 g
Fiber 2 g
Sugar 1.5 g
Protein 2 g

Low Carb Pound Cake

Preparation time: 10 minutes
Cooking time: 60 minutes
Servings: 12
Ingredients:
2 ½ cups almond flour
½ cup unsalted butter softened
1 ½ cups erythritol
8 whole eggs, room temperature
1 ½ teaspoons vanilla extract
½ teaspoon lemon extract
½ teaspoon salt
8 oz. cream cheese
1 ½ teaspoons baking powder

How to prepare:
Start by preparing and preheating the oven at 350 degrees F.
Beat cream cheese with erythritol and butter in a mixing bowl.
Whisk in vanilla extract, lemon extract, and eggs.
Beat well until smooth and fluffy.
Stir in baking powder, salt and almond flour then mix well.
Gradually add other ingredients and mix well.
Spread this batter in a loaf pan then bake for 60 minutes at 350 degrees F.
7.Slice and serve.

Nutritional Values:
Calories 155
Total Fat 13 g
Saturated Fat 5 g
Cholesterol 132 mg
Sodium 297 mg
Total Carbs 16 g
Fiber 2 g
Sugar 1.5 g
Protein 2 g

Conclusion

The word Ketogenic came into existence when experts discovered the importance of ketosis in human metabolism and how it can be enhanced to improve both the physical and mental health of a person. Thus experiments were conducted to determine the effects of carbohydrates and fats separately on the human body. Surprisingly, fats, when taken in isolation, proved to be far healthier than carbohydrates. It was discovered that these fats in the absence of carbohydrates are responsible for accelerating ketosis in the body. The idea of a ketogenic diet then witnessed a drastic increase in its popularity as the harms of the sugars or carbohydrates were brought forth to the world. In this cookbook, we shall see how to avoid those sugars in our daily routine while managing to enjoy similar flavors. Different sections of recipes are designed to provide a variety of bread, snacks, and desserts. Since avoiding flours and sugars are the toughest part of a ketogenic diet, these recipes are designed specially to keep those ingredients out of your life while giving you perfect substitutes.

www.ingramcontent.com/pod-product-compliance
Lightning Source LLC
Chambersburg PA
CBHW071733080526
44588CB00013B/2011